Teaching Teachers

Teaching Teachers

Bringing First-Rate Science to the Elementary Classroom

An NSTA Press Journals Collection

NATIONAL SCIENCE TEACHERS ASSOCIATION

Arlington, Virginia

NATIONAL SCIENCE TEACHERS ASSOCIATION

Claire Reinburg, Director
Judy Cusick, Associate Editor
Carol Duval, Associate Editor
Betty Smith, Associate Editor
Linda Olliver, Cover Design

ART AND DESIGN Linda Olliver, Director
NSTA WEB Tim Weber, Webmaster
PERIODICALS PUBLISHING Shelley Carey, Director
PRINTING AND PRODUCTION Catherine Lorrain-Hale, Director
    Nguyet Tran, Assistant Production Manager
    Jack Parker, Desktop Publishing Specialist
PUBLICATIONS OPERATIONS Erin Miller, Manager
sciLINKS Tyson Brown, Manager

NATIONAL SCIENCE TEACHERS ASSOCIATION
Gerald F. Wheeler, Executive Director
David Beacom, Publisher

Featuring sciLINKS®—a new way of connecting text and the Internet. Up-to-the-minute online content, classroom ideas, and other materials are just a click away. Go to page x to learn more about this new educational resource.

Printed in the USA by IPC Communications, Inc.
Printed on recycled paper.

02   5 4 3 2 1

Library of Congress Cataloging-in-Publication Data

Teaching teachers : bringing first-rate science to the elementary
classroom.
    p. cm.
"An NSTA Press journals collection."
Includes bibliographical references.
"NSTA stock number: PB167X"—T.p. verso.
ISBN 0-87355-203-2
    1. Science—Study and teaching (Elementary)—United States.   2. Science teachers—Training of—United States.   I. Title: Bringing first-rate science to the elementary classroom.   II. National Science Teachers Association.
LB1585.3 .T415 2002
372.3'5044—dc21

                                                                    2002003052
                                                                        CIP

Contents

Excellence for Every Teacher

Curriculum Integration

Assessment

Strategies for Every Day

Resources

Acknowledgments

The thirteen articles in *Teaching Teachers: How to Get First-Rate Science into the Elementary Classroom* all come from the "Teaching Teachers" column in *Science and Children*, NSTA's elementary school-level journal. The column was skillfully edited for many years by Michael Kotar, Science Education Department Head at California State University at Chico.

In addition to reviewing the articles, Maureen Beringer Moir, chair of NSTA's Pre-Service Teacher Preparation Committee and professor of science education and graduate coordinator of elementary education at Bridgewater State College, wrote the introduction and guided the organization. Committee members Julie Gess-Newsome, J. Lawrence Walkup Distinguished Professor of Science Education and Director of the Science and Math Learning Center at Northern Arizona State University, and Marsha Winegarner, director of District V 00-04 and Council Liaison 01-04 for the Florida Department of Education, also reviewed articles and made valuable suggestions.

Betty Smith was NSTA project editor for the book. Shelley Carey, director of periodicals, was instrumental in developing the book. Linda Olliver designed the cover, Nguyet Tran handled book layout, and Catherine Lorrain-Hale coordinated production and printing.

Introduction

The advent of educational reform and the publication of national standards in the various disciplines have brought new vitality and challenges to our nation's teachers. We, as science educators, welcomed the *National Science Education Standards* (National Academy Press 1996) as the guidelines for our activities in the 21st century.

In 1999, as part of its executive restructuring, the National Science Teachers Association (NSTA) replaced its Teacher Education Division with two new positions, Preservice Teacher Preparation and Professional Development. This action recognized the importance that the organization places on assisting teachers at various stages of their careers and the importance on supporting life-long learning.

"Teaching Teachers" has been a featured department in *Science and Children* for several years. It has included articles on issues in teacher education and staff development, discussions of curriculum development and assessment, and pieces on a wide variety of teaching strategies. The thirteen articles in this collection represent exemplary views and practices that support the Standards in practical situations.

The Standards address the need for teacher education at many stages of a teacher's career. It is suggested that teacher needs as learners be considered and built upon to increase confidence in science teaching and understanding of content.

The articles in the first section discuss two critical issues in science education reform. In the first, "Science is Part of the Big Picture," Greenwood discusses the need to convince already-busy experienced teachers that effective strategies are worth the time and effort required. In the second article, "Reaching the Reluctant Science Teacher," Colburn and Henriques present a preservice program for future teachers who feel unequipped to teach science.

Curriculum integration has become the cornerstone of educational reform. The Standards remind us that unifying concepts and processes give students strong ideas that help them better understand the natural world. These unifying concepts, when linked to other content or connected to other disciplines, can be used at any grade level. The Standards also remind us that teachers must put more emphasis on scientific concepts and the development of inquiry. The integration of all aspects of the science content in the context of technology, personal and social awareness is encouraged.

Section Two presents four models for curriculum integration. In "Curriculum Integration" Kotar et al. describe a preservice project for the development of a thematic unit in science with cross-curricula connections. One of the many strengths of this program is the fact that the preservice teachers actually develop the unit and test it during their field experiences.

Another model for use with preservice and practicing teachers focuses on the premise that the integration of technology into a science methods course can be valuable. In "STEPS into Learning," Sillman et al. emphasize the criticism of and dissatisfaction with traditional courses and describe a successful course that both acquaints students with several technological applications and increases their understanding of the teaching and learning of science. In another integrated model, French and Skochdopole present the use of the learning center in the study of a well-researched life cycle to teach preservice teachers in an engaging manner. "It's a Salmon's Life" incorporates several content Standards within the Standards and describes many cross-curricula applications suggested by the students and instructors.

In "Teaching Science When Your Principal Says Teach Language Arts," Akerson discusses the benefits of teaching practitioners to combine instruction in science and the language arts. She documents how students can write about science ideas in order to correct misconceptions and promote understanding.

More than ever, assessment is a critical part of the teaching and learning cycle. The Standards call for more authentic assessment of what is valued in our curriculum. Alternative assessment has become more popular in recent years. In Section Three, several forms of alternative or nontraditional assessment are discussed. In "Assessment for Preservice Teachers," Lehman suggests anecdotal observations, reflective journals and problem solving, integrated math and science data selection, and cooperative learning as possible assessment tools. In "Standards Direct Preservice Teaching Portfolios," Mosely describes an exemplary portfolio project for preservice teachers.

The final section of this collection features articles that suggest a wide variety of methods for use in preservice classes and staff development workshops. Some of these strategies are tried and true; others are newer or less known. All can be employed to enhance our application of the Standards.

In "Using Effective Demonstrations for Motivation," Freedman reminds us of the power of the use of a good demonstration or discrepant event in the elementary classroom. He also suggests that these demonstrations allow elementary students to see inquiry in action.

Few educators argue against the efficacy of hands-on science experiences. In "Managing Hands-on Inquiry," Rossman describes a survey in which there was a significant discrepancy between teacher beliefs and actual practice. His suggestions for a more effective approach are extremely valuable. Gay and Wilcox discuss another increasingly popular approach in "Science Discovery Centers." Preservice teachers design and present a center in which an appropriate topic is taught through interactive materials in actual school settings. A particularly effective part of this exercise is the adaptation of materials for age-appropriate groups and students of varying abilities.

Two especially challenging articles conclude this section. Bird describes the use of alternative modes of communication in "Talk Less, Say More." The author points out that this method affords her science-shy students special benefits and increased involvement. In "Never Give 'Em a Straight Answer," Ward suggests that educators should capitalize on the natural curiosity of students of all ages – and teach with careful questioning.

Our preservice and practicing teachers are among our nation's most valuable resources. Their ongoing professional development is critical. This collection suggests diverse ideas for consideration. All of them can be used to help us teach in the spirit of the promise expressed in the National Standards! "Teaching the Teachers" is still a rewarding and challenging task.

Maureen B. Moir, NSTA Teacher Preparation Director
Professor, Science Education, Bridgewater State College
February 2002

Teaching Teachers brings you *sci*LINKS, a new project that blends the two main delivery systems for curriculum—books and telecommunications—into a dynamic new educational tool for children, their parents, and their teachers. *sci*LINKS links specific science content with instructionally rich Internet resources. *sci*LINKS represents an enormous opportunity to create new pathways for learners, new opportunities for professional growth among teachers, and new modes of engagement for parents.

In this *sci*LINKed text, you will find an icon near several of the concepts being discussed. Under it, you will find the *sci*LINKS URL (*www.scilinks.org*) and a code. Go to the *sci*LINKS website, sign in, type the code from your text, and you will receive a list of URLs that are selected by science educators. Sites are chosen for accurate and age-appropriate content and good pedagogy. The underlying database changes constantly, eliminating dead or revised sites or simply replacing them with better selections. The *sci*LINKS search team regularly reviews the materials to which this text points, so you can always count on good content being available.

The selection process involves four review stages:

1. First, a cadre of undergraduate science education majors searches the World Wide Web for interesting science resources. The undergraduates submit about 500 sites a week for consideration.

2. Next, packets of these web pages are organized and sent to teacher-webwatchers with expertise in given fields and grade levels. The teacher-webwatchers can also submit web pages that they have found on their own. The teachers pick the jewels from this selection and correlate them to the National Science Education Standards. These pages are submitted to the *sci*LINKS database.

3. Scientists review these correlated sites for accuracy.

4. NSTA staff approve the web pages and edit the information provided for accuracy and consistent style.

*sci*LINKS is a free service for textbook and supplemental resource users, but obviously someone must pay for it. Participating publishers pay a fee to NSTA for each book that contains *sci*LINKS. The program is also supported by a grant from the National Aeronautics and Space Administration (NASA).

Science Is Part of the Big Picture

By Anita Greenwood

Recently, while leading a science workshop for elementary teachers, I experienced that "Aha!" moment of understanding that we educators always hope our students will have.

During a break, one workshop participant had described to me the demands being placed upon teachers in her school. "We are being told to use whole language, to try portfolio assessment, to teach hands-on science, to prepare thematic units, and to integrate mathematics and science," she said. "I don't even know where to start! There are so many things to do that it's like being asked to complete a jigsaw puzzle when each piece comes from a different puzzle and nothing seems to fit together." Her comments lead me to believe that I might finally understand one reason why inservice workshops often fail to have an impact on science teaching, and why even experienced teachers relegate science to the end of the day or avoid it altogether (McShane, 1995).

What Needs to Change?

Teachers consistently tell me that even though they know that letting children do hands-on science is beneficial, they nevertheless avoid teaching it or treat it as an add-on to the "core" of the elementary school curriculum. These teachers, typified by the workshop attendee who had given me such insight, do not see the links among the many new things they are being asked to incorporate into their teaching. Other workshop participants expressed the opinion that ideas presented to teachers during staff-development sessions are often just the latest fads, which tend to fizzle and die like spent firecrackers on the fourth of July. Then and there, I recognized that I, too, had failed to provide these teachers with the theoretical background that informs practice. In other words, I had launched into the "how to" of science teaching and had ignored the "why."

As a result, I restructured my workshop series so that teachers would become real science *learners*, struggling with their own ideas about the phases of the moon, seasons, living and non-living things, and so on as they designed experiments and shared theories with their peers. Teachers designed experiments to test their *own* ideas, and they discussed their old and new conceptions in relation to scientifically accepted models.

For example, in a workshop relating to density, teachers generated two competing ideas for why objects float and sink: objects float because they contain air, and objects sink because they have more mass than objects that float. To test their ideas, one group of teachers took jars and filled them with varying amounts of rocks until the jars sank; however, as everyone could see, the jars still contained air. Another group of teachers tested objects of the same mass but of different shape, and they discovered that mass alone was not the determining factor in sinking or floating. Working with their own ideas, teachers were more willing to search out alternative explanations, leading them eventually to conclude that while sinking and floating are related to mass and to the space taken up by an object, they are dependent on an object's density, which is reduced with the inclusion of air.

In another workshop, teachers kept a moon journal and generated a list of related "I wonder" questions, including

- I wonder where the moon is when I cannot see it;
- I wonder if the moon rotates, because I always seem to see the same face;
- and, I wonder what causes a lunar eclipse.

The teachers then explored each question through the use of models, working in a darkened room with an electric light representing the sun and a large plastic-foam ball on a wooden stick representing the moon. By holding the ball at arm's length and passing it around their own bodies, which represented Earth, the teachers were able to observe the reflection of light simulating the phases of the moon. This activity caused teachers to conclude that a lunar eclipse occurs every month! Knowing that this was not the case, the teachers used their models and further discussion to work out for themselves that the orbit of the moon around the Earth must be tilted with reference to the Earth's axis.

Through additional modeling and discussion, the teachers were able to resolve their conceptual difficulties related to the moon's phases and its rotation.

At the end of these redesigned workshops, we discussed what it was like to learn science and how that experience would affect their own classroom teaching. Through this new approach, teachers in my workshops began to recognize the "big picture" that frames the pedagogical changes they are being asked to implement.

Science Methods in Motion

If you believe that children are constantly attempting to explain all that they see and do, that they are trying to come up with theories about their world that make sense to them, then you already acknowledge that they are *active learners*. Active learning refers not only to physical activity, but also to mental activity. The teacher's role is to spark this mental activity by helping students connect what they already know with new experiences encountered in the classroom. This view of learning is part of the movement in science education known as *constructivism* (Driver and Oldham, 1986). When learning is recognized as a constructive activity, it provides a rationale for using cooperative grouping, alternative assessment, thematic teaching, and active learning in science.

The move toward thematic teaching acknowledges that children do not naturally categorize what they learn by subject; rather, they separate their knowledge into "little boxes" because of the way we organize the school day. By the time they reach high school, students so compartmentalize their learning that they don't relate the mathematics they learn during second period to the mathematics skills they need for their sixth-period science class! Making science part of a thematic or interdisciplinary unit helps students to forge appropriate connections and makes their learning more meaningful.

How, then, should we go about designing the science part of such interdisciplinary units? One way to start is by probing students' prior knowledge. Research has shown that students come to class with their own theories about how the world works (Asoko, 1993; Driver, Guesne, and Tiberghien, 1985). Such strategies as concept mapping, poster development, predict-observe-explain, line drawings, and sequence chains can elicit children's ideas (White and Gunstone, 1992), and then the teacher can focus instruction accordingly.

Most teachers believe that science lessons should involve students in inquiry, but they do not know how to change textbook exercises into active, challenging investigations. One ap-

This concept map shows how pedagogical ideas are linked.

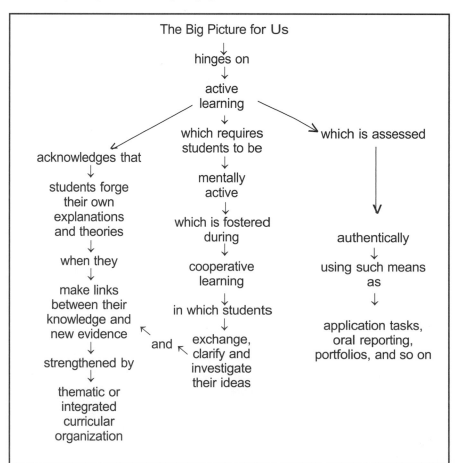

The Big Picture for Us
↓
hinges on
↓
active learning
↓   ↓
which requires   which is assessed
students to be
↓   ↓
acknowledges that   mentally
↓   active
students forge   ↓
their own   which is fostered   authentically
explanations   during   ↓
and theories   ↓   using such means
↓   cooperative   as
when they   learning   ↓
↓   ↓
make links   in which students   application tasks,
between their   ↓   oral reporting,
knowledge and   exchange,   portfolios, and so on
new evidence   and   clarify and
↓   investigate
strengthened by   their ideas
↓
thematic or
integrated
curricular
organization

proach is to rephrase as a question the title of a textbook exercise. In the primary grades, questions should lead to children developing their science process skills. The teacher might ask, for example, "What can you find out about feathers using a ruler, a hand lens, an eyedropper, a timer, and graph paper?" In grades 5–8, an appropriate question would be, "What factors affect how well lemonade crystals dissolve in water?"

Children should work cooperatively in groups to investigate these questions—exploring their ideas with peers, developing ways to test their thinking, and presenting findings from their data to the class. Activities that contradict children's misconceptions (identified by the teacher through the probing strategies described above) will lead students to question their prior understandings. From these initial explorations, students themselves generate more questions leading to further investigation.

Of course, there are questions that classroom investigations cannot answer. Such questions may become the subject of a student research project or a carry-over to their work in science the following year, or they may provide fodder for an e-mail conversation with a scientist.

Children should review their learning by revisiting the concept maps or other work they created at the beginning of a given unit of study and then revising these materials in light of what they've learned. This gives students concrete evidence of their learning and provides the teacher with a useful assessment tool.

Finally, there is little point in encouraging students to think, share, investigate and develop explanations if they are only going to fill in the blanks on a test sheet. Instead, teachers should use authentic assessment, in which students can apply their learning and teachers can evaluate their performance—to what degree they follow directions, organize the data they collect, use measuring instruments appropriately and accurately, and develop explanations for their observations. In addition, portfolios are an excellent way for students to select evidence and maintain a record of their developing skills and knowledge.

Teachers as Learners

Once I had restructured my workshops so that the attending teachers experienced science as *learners* would, workshop participants began to consider changing their own instructional strategies. They recognized that when their ideas were challenged and sometimes shown to be false, the teachers became intensely interested in their learning. Additionally, workshop attendees saw how the pedagogy advocated in a variety of professional development workshops assisted them in learning science. For example, cooperative learning is more than a grouping strategy; it provides an atmosphere conducive to the exchange of ideas and to inquiry.

By becoming active learners themselves, these teachers recognized that science is part of the "big picture," and they were able to link newly constructed ideas about active learning to other pedagogical initiatives (see figure). At the same time, I learned a valuable lesson, too: that I must not neglect theory if the teachers I train are to develop a model that assists them in modifying their instructional approaches and makes sense of professional development activities.

Resources

Asoko, H. (1993). First steps in the construction of a theoretical model of light: A case study from a primary school classroom. *Proceedings of the Third International Seminar on Misconceptions in Science and Mathematics Education.* Ithaca, NY: Misconceptions Trust.

Driver, R., Guesne, E., and Tiberghien, A. (Eds.). (1985). *Children's ideas in science.* Milton Keynes, United Kingdom: Open University Press.

Driver, R., and Oldham, V. (1986). A constructivist approach to curriculum development in science. *Studies in Science Education, 13,* 105–122.

Grennon Brooks, J., and Brooks, M. (1993). *In search of understanding: The case for constructivist classrooms.* Alexandria, VA: Association for Supervision and Curriculum Design.

McShane, J. (1995). Editor's note: Science is a priority. *Science and Children, 32*(4), 4.

White, R., and Gunstone, R. (1992). *Probing understanding.* Bristol, PA: The Falmer Press, Taylor and Francis.

ANITA GREENWOOD is an assistant professor of science education at the University of Massachusetts Lowell.

Reaching the
Reluctant Science Teacher

By Alan Colburn and Laura Henriques

"I don't like science!" "I don't know enough science to teach it." "I don't know *how* to teach inquiry-based science!" As a science educator, you've probably heard many reasons why someone is reluctant to teach science. You may have even shared some of these feelings yourself. A Process Approach to Science, a science course we designed at California State University–Long Beach, aims to change these attitudes and abilities. Students enrolled in the course include juniors and seniors studying to be elementary teachers who have already completed one life, one Earth, and one physical science course. For many students, this is the last science course they will take before entering the classroom.

A Process Approach to Science is a *science* class not a *methods* class, and students receive *science* credit upon its completion. Students spend the majority of their class time conducting hands-on, inquiry-based activities, while outside of class they read pedagogical literature about elementary-level teaching. As instructors, we model teaching and assessment methods that students will likely use in their elementary classroom and that are consistent with our course goals.

While modeling appropriate methods is an important aspect of the course, it is the interplay between content and pedagogy that truly makes this course unique. The following describes how we blend these elements in several of the units in the course.

Hands-On, Minds-On Science

We begin the semester with a small unit in which students investigate pendulums using only string and washers. Students are challenged to create an object that will swing back and forth 60 times in one minute, and then investigate their ideas on how factors like weight and string length affect the pendulum's period. We don't provide students with any guidelines about the length of the string or number of washers to use to conduct the study. The students must create the pendulum on their own.

After completing these activities during class, students read an article about the advantages of hands-on, minds-on science as homework (Graika, 1989). A brief course discussion then relates hands-on science to the activity students just finished. Students then contrast "hands-on" and

"hands-on, minds-on" activities, and explain why the pendulum unit was "hands-on, minds-on." Most students already recognize the value of a hands-on activity; however, they still must learn to discern step-by-step cookbook activities from open-ended, or "minds-on" ones. The open-ended nature of their exploration of the pendulums helps students recognize the difference.

Understanding the Nature of Science

Next, students complete a Mystery Powders unit that introduces elementary chemistry and qualitative analysis. In this unit students determine the contents of an unknown white powder. As they did in the pendulum unit, students read about a related pedagogical topic outside of class—in this case, the nature of science (Spurlin, 1995).

Being open-ended, this unit provides many opportunities for instructors to point out parallels between students' experiences and the nature of science. For example, students generally use different procedures to identify the unknown powder. We always point this out to the class,

National Science Teachers Association

ALL PHOTOGRAPHS COURTESY OF THE AUTHOR

emphasizing the idea that though the procedures were different, they still solved the same problem—determining the contents of the powder.

The importance of evidence in science is another major point emphasized in the unit. Numerous questions asked during the unit such as "How do you know?" "Are you sure?" or "What would it take for you to be more confident in your conclusion?" help students understand this key element of science.

Although students read literature about the nature of science and we conduct brief follow-up discussions in class, it is the situations that arise from their hands-on experiences that provide the best places for learning about this topic.

To end the unit students complete a quiz that reflects both their understanding of the nature of science and

their powder-identification expertise. Students must respond to various scenarios that illustrate aspects of the nature of science. They describe how an activity is like "real science" or what role new evidence plays in their analysis. Additionally, they must identify unknown powders and use data from their laboratory books to support their conclusions.

Developing Experimental Know-How

Another important part of this course is teaching students how to conduct scientific research. Throughout the course they participate in activities designed to help them understand the kinds of decisions scientists make when devising procedures and interpreting data.

To develop their science-research skills, students as a class investigate a

question about a variable affecting plant growth. Each student cares for an individual plant, and the class data is pooled. For example, students might choose to investigate how motor oil in soil affects plant growth. Our job as instructors is to promote student thinking by asking questions about aspects of the experiment's design, then let the class collectively figure out responses.

Later, during another unit students generate researchable questions to answer themselves. Usually this occurs within the context of studying a small animal like the mealworm or pillbug. Students generally investigate how the animals respond to different environmental factors, such as temperature range, intensity of light, or amount of moisture. As with the other units, students read articles related to the teaching strategies they are expe-

Teaching Teachers Excellence for Every Teacher   **5**

riencing (Shiland, 1997).

Students also develop their investigation skills by testing consumer products to determine which brand is "best." This assignment teaches students about the concepts of fair testing, variable control, and multiple trials to establish confidence in results. For example, a student testing how much weight a paper plate could hold would probably make sure to place her weight on each plate in the same place, in the same manner, while holding the edges of each plate at the same places. In addition to their in-class activities, students read articles by teachers who have conducted consumer-testing activities with elementary students (Rosenzweig, 1995).

Toward the end of the semester students conduct their own independent science investigations. They create researchable questions, devise repeatable procedures, collect and analyze data, write reports, and share results. In addition, students are required to investigate a second question that arose from the first experiment. This part of the assignment helps counteract the incorrect notion that science experiments are a cut-and-dried process, with scientists answering questions with single (experimental) procedures. In truth, the questions and answer seeking continue forever, with one tentative conclusion simply opening the door to new investigations.

Exploring Misconceptions and Conceptual Change

We use the Floating and Sinking unit to introduce students to Piagetian thought. Students study Piaget's work and learn the general distinction between abstract concepts and concrete ideas. While completing density and buoyancy explorations in class and doing assigned readings, students must also interview elementary children regarding their ability to *conserve* (one of Piaget's broad thinking structures). In this context, conservation refers to recognizing when something has remained the same. For example, spreading out a group of pennies does not change the number of pennies, or pouring a glass of water into an empty tub does not change the liquid's volume. Young children have often not yet developed these cognitive abilities. We help preservice teachers see that if their students lack the ability to conserve some quantities, their students will be unable to acquire a deep understanding of the concepts of density and buoyancy.

Students also complete a unit on electric circuits, which also accents the distinctions between abstract concepts and concrete ideas (National Science Resources Center, 1991). Through this unit, preservice teachers understand that studying electrical circuits represents a concrete idea and is best suited for the elementary grades. Ideas like voltage and current, on the other hand, are more abstract and better left for introduction in later grades.

Both units introduce students to misconceptions and conceptual change. By maintaining an emphasis on conceptual change during the unit, students generally come to understand the misconceptions they once had about the nature of density and/or electrical circuits. Students create and maintain KWL charts during the units, determine their own rules for sinking and floating or what makes a bulb light, and have their ideas challenged. Emphasizing the major concepts as stated in the *National Science Education Standards* (National Research Council, 1996) instead of focusing on abstract ideas increases the chance that conceptual change will occur in our students. Since they undergo some degree of conceptual

change themselves, students find it easy to see how their future students will change ideas when confronting new evidence, too.

Science Teachers, All of Us

We designed this course with the reluctant prospective elementary science teacher in mind. Positive experiences in a single science course may not be enough to make some students eager about teaching science. We recognize this and have devised a strategy to help them. Students in our class keep a comprehensive journal. They list all materials used during investigations, procedures, results, data analysis, and conclusions. We want students to leave the class feeling comfortable with at least one or two of the units they completed during the semester. Armed with their journals, they can then try just one or two of these units with their classes in the near future. They will then see for themselves how excited elementary school children get when busy with good science lessons!

We also provide students with a list of suppliers and resources for all the materials used during the course. This eliminates the excuse of not knowing where to get materials. Many former students have called or e-mailed us after teaching in their own classroom to ask for a replacement list.

All students can identify and describe attributes of elementary teachers who like science. It is our hope that they will be able to relate to some of those attributes and to incorporate some of these traits into their teaching.

Alan Colburn is an associate professor of science education, and Laura Henriques is an assistant professor, both at California State University–Long Beach.

Resources

Carey, S.S. (1994). *A Beginner's Guide to Scientific Method.* Belmont, CA: Wadsworth.

Consuegra, G.F., and Hetherington, J. (1991). A change of pace. *Science and Children, 28*(7), 13–15.

Graika, T. (1989). Minds-on, hands-on science. *Science Scope, 12*(6), 18–20.

Kotar, M. (1989). Demystifying mystery powders. *Science and Children, 26*(6), 25–28.

National Research Council. (1996). *National Science Education Standards.* Washington, DC: National Academy Press.

National Science Resources Center. (1991). *Electric Circuits.* Burlington, NC: Carolina Biological Supply.

Phillips, D. (1981). Chemistry for the elementary school. *Science and Children, 19*(2), 8–12.

Rosenzweig, B. (1995). Consumer reports classroom style. *Science and Children, 32*(3), 20–23, 32.

Shiland, T.W.(1997). Decookbook it! *Science and Children, 34*(3), 14–18.

Spurlin, Q. (1995). Put science in a bag. *Science and Children, 32*(4), 19–22.

Curriculum

By Michael Kotar,
Cris E. Guenter,
Devon Metzger, and
James L. Overholt

Integration:

A Teacher Education Model

In a unique course at our university, preservice teachers learn about interdisciplinary education and curriculum development by actually creating an integrated instructional unit. The rationale for this course is based on the belief that, "Teachers who develop interdisciplinary curriculums with their students are affirming that they are scholars in their own right, reinventing their practice as they interact with their students and engage them with increasingly complex content within changing instructional settings and situations." (Martinello and Cook, 1994, p. 4). This course gives preservice teachers the valuable opportunity to assume leadership roles in implementing curriculum integration.

The foundation for this course is built in the preservice teachers' previous content methods courses and field experiences. The faculty of the science, mathematics, social studies, and arts methods courses use a single combined syllabus. Language arts methods and multicultural education also build connections to the core content areas.

Laying the Groundwork

To begin the course, we facilitate discussions that explain and clarify the rationale for curriculum integration. It cannot be overstated how important it is to work with students to carefully examine the rationale for curriculum integration.

We distribute integrated thematic unit directions to help guide, clarify, and standardize the unit development process (see Figure 1) and present planning models, such as concept mapping and webbing. We use the actual process of planning this university course as a realistic model, discussing the frustrations, spirited debates, challenges, and successes involved in this collaborative experience. The effect for many preservice teachers is a discovery experience—an awakening to the possibilities of problem-based interdisciplinary education.

To conclude the introduction, we share sample units that model curriculum integration with the students. Typically, these model units are the exemplary units developed by students from previous semesters.

Developing Integrated Units

Following the introduction to curriculum integration, preservice teachers begin the important task of forming groups. Because group dynamics are so critical to effective curriculum planning, course time is allotted for helping preservice teachers make decisions about forming their teams, including considerations such as lifestyles, personal schedules, work habits, travel time, and personalities. This process can take several days.

The newly formed teams then select a unit topic, theme, or problem to solve. In the struggle to reach a consensus, compromise is usually necessary. This process of decision making often predicts the eventual quality of the integrated unit. It is not uncommon for at least one group to show the stresses of group interaction and group decision making in this initial planning stage.

As the teams begin preparing their units in class, the seminars become planning sessions, and the instructors serve as "resource colleagues." During these early working sessions, it is sometimes necessary to help teams focus or narrow their selected topic. Early intervention helps prevent unit development problems.

We provide a checklist of general unit expectations and requirements (Figure 2) that will be used as a guide-

Problem-based interdisciplinary units are challenging for both teachers and students. Here, students prepare displays during an endangered species study.

Figure 1. Steps for Planning Integrated Thematic Instructional Units.

These steps form one approach for planning an instructional unit. Use the directions as listed, modify them, or apply your own experience and knowledge to create a system for unit development that meets your own interests and curriculum needs.

Step 1: Identify the topic/theme, a rationale that supports the topic/theme, and intended learning outcomes for students. Include learning skills among the outcomes you select. Ask: What skills and knowledge do I want my students to acquire? What topics/themes/ideas must I address in my curriculum? Use your understanding of the interests and needs of students you are teaching to help you identify topics/themes. Interviewing learners can help assess interest, relevance, and understanding. Curriculum frameworks, district and grade level curriculum guides, and teacher manuals can also help identify topics/themes/ideas.

Step 2: List and analyze any ideas you have about the topic/theme. Use a system designed for this purpose such as webbing, concept mapping, question generation and categorizing, or the concentric circle model. List related ideas and explore pathways and connections. Often, exemplary instructional units and interesting studies are created by following what appear at first to be minor ideas.

Step 3: Conduct further research on the topic/theme. Find information and locate resources for instructional activities.

Step 4: Identify appropriate instructional strategies and activities. Investigations of all types are especially appropriate when you are trying to facilitate acquisition of learning skills and ideas about the topic/theme. Especially important is the development of learning activities that help students conduct investigations. These may include library research, interviews of experts, visits to museums, and similar activities in addition to the data-gathering investigations of science and mathematics.

Step 5: Identify and select materials you will need in order to teach the unit. Be prepared to modify instructional activities to use materials that are readily available.

Step 6: Write an organized plan for your integrated thematic unit. Focus on the "big picture" while remaining aware of the problems being solved in each content area.

Figure 2. Unit Expectations and Requirements.

Required Components

❑ **Unit Identification.** Include topic/theme title, grade level(s) or age levels, projected time of unit duration.

❑ **Rationale.** A rationale offers a justification for decisions made about content or process to educators, parents, students, and you. A rationale answers such questions as, "Why are children being required to know this subject, learn this skill, develop this attitude, or experience learning in this fashion?"

❑ **Unit Outline or Overview.** A number of options exist in your approach to this requirement. An outline can show chronological arrangement of the unit, main ideas, and/or student outcomes. Outlines can also be arranged to serve as tables of contents. An overview may be narrative and/or include lists to describe concepts, learning processes, and skills, along with student outcomes and instructional approaches. Consider creating a document that will be useful in describing the unit to another person.

❑ **Web, Concept Map, or List.** Include a copy of the planning approach used to help generate, organize, and make connections between ideas in your unit.

❑ **Goals and Objectives List.** A clearly written list of instructional goals and objectives for the unit should be included. Keep in mind that goals are global and objectives are operational. Objectives should be listed under each goal, demonstrating the connection and application of the objectives to the accompanying goal. It is recommended that objectives be taken directly from the lesson plans developed by your group.

❑ **Brief Narrative of the Planning Steps.** Include a description of planning successes and difficulties, similar to a journal entry. Document and reflect on what worked well and not-so-well for your group.

❑ **Lesson Plans.** Your group's integrated thematic unit requires a minimum of five lesson plans in at least three curricular areas. All lesson plans must be specifically designed for the unit and written in a consistent format that includes rationale, objectives, introduction, procedures, closure, materials, and evaluation. Lesson plans photocopied from teacher manuals or guides will not be accepted. It is acceptable (and a wise use of time) to use teacher guides and manuals as resources for activities to be included in lessons.

❑ **Supplemental Components.** Include a wide range of teaching possibilities such as teacher manual references, a letter to parents, a list of trade books, bulletin board plans, a vocabulary activity, a computer activity, a laser disk activity, transparencies, a field trip, resource speakers, a writing activity, a game, extra lesson plans, related information accessed on the Internet, and so on.

Presentation Score

The presentation score will be based on the following criteria:
❑ appropriateness and sufficiency of unit information,
❑ clarity of communication,
❑ participation of group members,
❑ involvement and participation of audience,
❑ and creativity/interest of presentation.

Group Evaluation

The individual's evaluation by the group will be based on the following criteria:
❑ attendance at planned meetings;
❑ preparation for presentation;
❑ contributions to positive group dynamics (being helpful, supportive, constructive, and conscientious);
❑ encouraging others to present their ideas (not dominating or intimidating group peers);
❑ and overall contribution to the group.

line for final unit evaluation. Group progress meetings help us to check the developing units and provide needed opportunities for troubleshooting, offering individual and group support and encouragement, and sharing our expertise.

On the final day of the course, teams present a 40–45 minute overview of their prepared units to the course instructors and their student peers. Typically, these presentations are creatively done and include ways for the audience to learn about the goals, objectives, and organization of the unit. The audience often participates in selected unit activities and lessons. Presentations are open to other faculty and public school colleagues. These public presentations allow for peer and faculty review, the sharing of collected resources, course closure, and valuable public relations opportunities.

Many students use their classroom connections to help them with unit development, surveying children to determine "natural" questions about topics. Later, it is common for the units to be taught during student teaching. Several students have been invited to present their units at conferences, including regional science teaching conferences and district professional development days.

Units are evaluated by faculty and peers based on the presentations and overall quality. Preservice teachers also provide a written self-evaluation of how their team worked to assess the overall unit development process and individual accountability within the team.

A Renewed Approach

Integrating the curriculum is a renewed approach to teaching and learning that more closely resembles how people learn and work in the real world. The belief that "the whole is more than the sum of the parts" is a powerful curriculum movement that is helping children make learning connections. Likewise, this integrated curriculum course allows preservice teachers to initiate, design, plan, develop, and present an integrated unit that is immediately useful in the school classroom.

Resources

California State Department of Education. (1992). *It's Elementary!* Sacramento: Author.

Charbonneau, M., and Reider, B. (1995). *The Integrated Elementary Classroom: A Developmental Model of Education for the 21st Century.* Boston: Allyn and Bacon.

Frazee, B., and Rudnitski, R. (1995). *Integrated Teaching Methods.* New York: Delmar.

Kohn, A. (1994). The truth about self-esteem. *Phi Delta Kappan, 75*(4), 281–282.

Martinello, M., and Cook, G. (1994). *Interdisciplinary Inquiry in Teaching and Learning.* New York: Merrill.

Roberts, P., and Kellough, R. (1996). *A Guide for Developing an Interdisciplinary Thematic Unit.* Englewood Cliffs, NJ: Prentice-Hall.

MICHAEL KOTAR, CRIS E. GUENTER, DEVON METZGER, and JAMES L. OVERHOLT are all professors in the Department of Science Education at California State University, Chico.

STEPS into Learning

Prospective elementary teachers explore the use of classroom technologies in a university setting

By Kathleen Sillman, Carla Zembal-Saul, and Thomas M. Dana

"I HAD A BLAST! I LEARNED a lot about motion and temperature, especially because we got to do it on computers!" "The third-grade students could really understand the concepts; the technology really enhanced the lesson!" "I gained confidence in teaching with technology!"

These were some of the typical comments we heard during STEPS (Science and Technology Experiences at Penn State) Days, a unique event for prospective teachers that integrated technology into inquiry-based science. In essence, the event was a "reverse field experience." Instead of university students visiting elementary classrooms to practice teaching, this program brought elementary students to the university, where prospective elementary teachers team-taught technology-enhanced science lessons. For many, this event was both

their first science teaching experience with technology and their first inquiry lesson. Overall, the prospective teachers gained confidence in how to teach inquiry-based science with technology and felt better prepared as they looked ahead to teaching technology-enhanced science lessons in their future classrooms.

Why This Course Is Needed

A common concern in teacher education is that prospective teachers do not find their teacher preparation courses helpful (Calderhead and Robson, 1991; Kagan, 1992; Zeichner and Gore, 1990). They typically feel the courses are "'too theoretical' and have no bearing on what 'real' teachers do in 'real' classrooms with 'real' students" (p. 190, Bransford, Brown, and Cocking, 1999). As a result, prospective teachers generally fail to see a viable connection between theory and practice.

The *National Science Education Standards* (National Research Council, 1996) emphasize more meaningful professional development within both preservice and inservice programs. Among other things, quality programs are characterized by "options that recognize the developmental nature of teacher professional growth" that "can be built over time, reinforced continuously, and practiced in a variety of situations" (p. 70, National Research Council, 1996). The *Standards* also advocate that learning experiences for teachers of science "must occur in a variety of places where effective science teaching can be illustrated and modeled, permitting teachers to struggle with real situations and expand their knowledge and skills in appropriate contexts" (p. 62, National Research Council, 1996).

A significant part of the context of any science education program is

Preservice teachers test their teaching skills as they instruct elementary students in using various microcomputer-based laboratories.

technology. Within the *National Science Education Standards* (National Research Council, 1996), technology is viewed as "tools that help scientists make better observations, measurements, and equipment for investigations" to help them "see, measure, and do things they could not otherwise see, measure, and do" (p. 138, National Research Council, 1996).

Certainly, science learning is more effective when it resembles authentic science practice, and at the heart of authentic science practice are the tools and resources technology can provide (Brodie et al., 1992). One tool that helps scientists display and analyze data is probeware, a type of microcomputer-based lab (MBL). Findings suggest that the MBLs supported children's understandings and abilities to interpret graphs largely by eliminating laborious graphing procedures (Nakhleh, 1994).

Consistent with the *Standards*, teacher preparation programs need to expose prospective teachers to a range of computer technology in methods and content courses that emphasize technology as a strategy for teachers to support children's scientific inquiry and conceptual learning. As with other strategies, to effectively use technology, many teachers need to have these learning experiences illustrated and modeled within appropriate contexts.

STEPS Overview

STEPS Days effectively accomplished all of these goals. STEPS Days were part of a larger effort at the university to integrate technology into an inquiry-based program of science learning and teaching. The primary purpose of the program was to help prospective elementary teachers learn science through technology and become proficient in its use so that they can then teach technology-enhanced science lessons to elementary students, first at the university and then within their field experience classrooms.

To begin the program, prospective teachers learned how to use three microcomputer-based laboratory technologies involving motion, heart rate, and temperature sensors that are typically used in elementary classrooms. Early in the semester, methods instructors demonstrated how to use the probeware technology (we used PASCO Science Workshop [1998] software with curriculum modifications appropriate for elementary learners as well as Tom Snyder's The Graph Club [1999]). In two-hour blocks of time, teachers were taught how to use a motion sensor to explore the concept of sonar, how it works, and its uses; a heart-rate sensor to predict heart rate changes during various activities; and a temperature probe to predict freezing point differences among various mixtures and solutions.

Once the teachers felt comfortable using the probeware themselves, they began planning lessons for the STEPS event. About two weeks before the scheduled event, the teachers broke into three large groups (one group for each kind of sensor) to discuss how to teach elementary students each concept using the probeware. After these large brainstorming sessions, the three groups broke into smaller teaching teams of three to five people to create lessons for particular grade levels. For a homework assignment, each team created a lesson plan to use during the STEPS event.

In the next class (a two-hour block), the teams practiced teaching their lesson first within their group and then later in front of the

With immediate graphing generated by the computer, students could concentrate more on the interpretation and understanding of the science concept.

whole class. The teachers used the practice sessions to troubleshoot problems with the lessons and to revise them. At this point, the teachers were ready to teach the lessons to the elementary students.

Teaching "Real" Students

When STEPS Day came, elementary students and their teachers arrived from local elementary schools within a 45-minute drive to the university. To choose the participating schools, we contacted superintendents, principals, and science supervisors through letters and telephone calls and asked if they were interested in participating in the program. The first five schools that volunteered were chosen, representing students from grades two to six. The event lasted about four hours.

When the elementary students arrived, they were divided into small groups of two to four students. Students experienced a lesson at three different microcomputer-based laboratory stations—Mapping the Ocean Floor (motion sensor), Heart Rate Comparisons (heart rate sensor), and Ice Cream Making (temperature sensor). At each lab station the student-to-teacher ratio was one-to-one with three to four teachers and two to four elementary students. Students stayed at each station about 25–35 minutes.

Prospective teachers taught one lesson at each station, and the activities were adjusted slightly to fit the level of the students. Typically, teachers introduced the probeware by asking questions such as, "Have you ever seen anything like this?" and "What do you think it does?" In several instances, teachers chose student volunteers to operate the computer and then guided them to the appropriate areas on the screen to click.

For example, at the Mapping the Ocean Floor station, elementary students used the probe to map an "ocean floor" made from boxes of different sizes. The sensor emits ultrasonic pulses and detects pulses returned as echoes from the target. When students passed the motion sensor over the terrain of boxes, the software then created an inverted graph that the teachers guided students in interpreting. The lesson concluded as students challenged peers to form the floor as indicated by the graph.

At the Heart Rate Comparison station, elementary students used the heart-rate sensor to compare their heart rates at rest and at various levels of activity. The students predicted answers to the question, "Which activity will produce a higher heart rate, running or jumping?" and then tested their predictions.

At the Ice Cream Making station, students used the temperature probe as part of the process of making a frozen treat. Using the probe, students measured the temperature of the ice-water surrounding a container of ice cream ingredients and predicted how the temperature would be affected when salt was added to the water. Most students thought there would be no change in temperature when the salt was added. After the students added the salt to the ice water, they again measured the temperature with the probe and observed an immediate drop in temperature.

This observation naturally led to questions and further observations as students became immersed in the inquiry. Some students wondered, "Why did the temperature of the water drop after the salt was added? How low did the temperature go before the milk became ice cream?" The probe temperature readings of the ice cream that students took both before and after becoming a solid were key pieces of scientific evidence in their discussions as students enjoyed the tasty results of their efforts!

Because each teaching team taught the lesson three times (so that each group of elementary students could experience all three stations), each prospective elementary teacher was able to experience the role of teacher, observer of children's thinking, and manager of details. The "teacher" focused on the delivery of the lesson from an inquiry perspective. The "observer" paid particular attention to the meanings of the various science concepts that individual students constructed. The "manager" operated the video recorder, helped students prepare their nametags, awarded stickers upon completion of the lesson, and provided the snack.

Benefits for Prospective Teachers

Prospective teachers valued the experience for several reasons. For most, the experience of team teaching was new. The benefit of team teaching was that each prospective teacher had a chance to experience a different role each time the lesson was taught. They compared and contrasted their individual experiences. One commented on the value of being the observer, "Working with small groups of children, I could really hear the questions each individual had. It was easier to observe them."

Prospective teachers seemed to agree that technology was a motivator for learning. One teacher commented, "I could see the excitement in the students' eyes while using the technology!" However, prospective teachers also seemed to differentiate between the novelty of technology as a motivator and technology as an enhancement for understanding science concepts.

One teacher who used the probeware articulated best what many of the participating colleagues voiced, "The technology acted as a tool, not the teacher. The computer generated the graphs and the visualizations seemed to help the students understand the concepts." Because the computer provided the graphs, prospective teachers felt the visualization tool provided immediate graphing that allowed elementary students to concentrate more on the interpretation and understanding of the science concept. The value of the probeware to enhance meaningful understanding of science concepts was unanimous among prospective teachers.

Conclusions

Overall, this program did more than to introduce essential technology to prospective elementary teachers of science. Bringing "real" elementary students to the science methods classes helped prospective teachers see how technology can be used effectively with students. In addition, the visiting practicing teachers can also be introduced to use this technology to teach science. Most importantly, the visiting students learned some science concepts, and they also had fun and were motivated to learn. One elementary student summed it up, "It was the best field trip ever!"

Kathleen Sillman is an assistant professor of education, Carla Zembal-Saul is an assistant professor of education, and Thomas M. Dana is an associate professor of education, all at The Pennsylvania State University in Julian.

Resources
Print

Bransford, J.D., Brown, A.L., and Cocking, R.R. (1999*). How People Learn: Brain, Mind, Experience, and School.* Washington, DC: National Academy Press.

Brodie, K.W., Carpenter, L.A., Earnshaw, R.A., Gallop, J.R., Hubbold, R.J., Mumford, A.M., Osland, C.D., and Quarendon, P. (1992). *Scientific Visualization.* Berlin, Germany: Springer-Verlag.

Calderhead, J., and Robson, M. (1991). Images of teaching: Student teachers' early conceptions of classroom practice. *Teaching and Teacher Education, 7*(1), 1–8.

Friedrichsen, P., Sillman, K., Dana, T., and Zembal-Saul, C. (2000). Integrating technology into the science teacher education program. Paper presented at the Teaching and Learning with Technology Symposium, The Pennsylvania State University, University Park, Pennsylvania.

Kagan, D.M. (1992). Professional growth among preservice beginning teachers. *Review of Educational Research, 62,* 129–169.

Nakhleh, M.B. (1994). A review of microcomputer-based labs: How have they affected science learning? *Journal of Computers in Mathematics and Science Teaching, 13,* 368–381.

National Research Council. (1966). *National Science Education Standards.* Washington, DC: National Academy Press.

Zeichner, K.M., and Gore, J.M. (1990). Teacher socialization. In W.R. Houston (Ed.), *Handbook of Research on Teacher Education* (pp. 329–348). New York: MacMillan.

Internet

ScienceWorkshop [probeware and software program]. (1998). PASCO Scientific. http://www.pasco.com.

The Graph Club [software program]. (1999). Tom Snyder Productions. http://www.tomsnyder.com.

Also in S&C

Lough, T., and Mills, E. (1999). Day of science. *Science and Children, 37*(3), 40–44.

It's a Salmon's Life!

By M. Jenice French and Laura Downey Skochdopole

Making science exciting and rigorous for children and adults is a primary goal of science educators. But many preservice elementary teachers are anxious about science. So, we decided to immerse preservice teachers—cognitively, affectively, and kinesthetically—into an integrated science unit to help them gain confidence in their abilities to learn and teach science.

In this unit, preservice teachers took on the role of a salmon as they learned about the salmon's life cycle and the difficulties salmon encounter. For a hands-on context, we used a series of activity stations (see Salmon Activity Stations box). The stations were divided into three phases: Going Out to Sea, At Sea, and Back Upstream. We also included two Wait Stations. The stations were set up in various parts of the room according to the three phases. Each station was identified with a letter to ensure that the teachers completed them in the proper sequence. Each station included the directions and materials needed to conduct the activity.

As the teachers progressed through the stations, they were faced with a variety of simulated hazards. For example, at the first station, the teachers used a radish rubbing to test the pH of various liquids representing streams. At another station, the teachers tried to navigate through a twirling jump rope that simulated turbine blades near a dam. The wait stations were used while the groups were waiting to begin their journey and when groups had extra time after completing a station.

A preservice teacher measures the pH of various liquids representing streams.

Salmon Activity Stations

Going Out to Sea

Station A: Can You Survive the pH Level of the Stream?

This station explores the dangers of unsafe pH levels in rivers and streams due to water pollution. Each "school" will need

- six numbered containers of liquid that may be neutral, acidic, or basic (We used four containers with water only, one container of diluted vinegar or lemon juice, and one container of diluted bleach or ammonia.);
- a radish;
- index cards;
- a die (from a board game);
- and eyedroppers.

Directions: Each container of liquid represents a stream. With members of your school, discuss how the pH of a liquid indicates the presence of an acid or a base. Rub the radish on an index card until a stain is evident. One by one, each "salmon" should roll a die, then test water from that "stream" by placing two drops on the radish rubbing. A color change to bright pink indicates an acid and a change to blue Indicates a base. If you see no change, then the stream you are in is safe and you can continue your journey. If you see a color change, the stream you are in is not suitable for life and you should mark your death on your life cycle chart.

Station B: Fishing for Fate

This station explores a variety of potential hazards that salmon encounter on their way downstream. The materials include

- a "fishing pole" made of a dowel rod with a string tied to one end and a magnet tied to the string;
- and fate cards (see Figure 1), each with a paper clip attached, placed in a bucket.

Directions. Using the fishing pole, fish for a fate card in the bucket. Read your fate aloud to the members of your school. Retain your card until everyone in your school is done fishing, then return all cards to the bucket. If you die, record your death on your life cycle chart.

Station C: The Turbines

As salmon travel toward the last leg of their journey downstream, they encounter problems with turbine blades near dams. This station uses a twirling jump rope to simulate that challenge.

Directions: While two colleagues twirl the jump rope, try to pass through it without touching the rope or becoming entangled. You may pass straight through or jump, as long as the "turbine blade" doesn't touch you.

Station D: Fishing for Fate

Again, the salmon must fish for their fate. Materials and directions are the same as for Station B.

At Sea

Before proceeding, we bring together all of the salmon and explain that, if they are still alive at this point, they have made it to the sea where they may spend several years of their life as adult salmon. The salmon share their survival data with the other schools, develop a classroom graph of survival, and discuss patterns of mortality related to the stations completed. But the journey isn't over!

Station D: Fisherman's Maze

At sea, fishers, seals, whales, and sea birds pose a common threat to salmon. This station simulates being caught in a fisher's net and trying to escape. We provided photocopied fish mazes (a maze we had drawn with a salmon at one end and open waters on the other).

Directions: This is an all-group activity, however, only those preservice teachers surviving the previous stations should be tracked in the data collected. Each salmon must complete the maze within 30 seconds in order to escape and continue the journey.

Back Upstream

Station E: Bearangerous!

When hundreds of salmon gather at the mouth of a river on their way back home to spawn, predators, such as bears and otters, use this gathering time as an opportunity for easy fishing. This game is adapted from "Salmon Run," a problem-solving activity in *Family Math* (Stenmark, Thompson, and Cossey, 1991). The materials needed are

- several streams drawn on paper with spaces for the salmon to move a single leap at a time and rocks for the bear (see Stenmark, Thompson, and Cossey, 1991 for further instructions and stream drawings);
- and bean seeds, to use as game pieces to represent the salmon and the bear.

Directions: In this game, the salmon still alive within your school will attempt to swim past a bear, played by a no-longer-living member of your school. The bear sits on a rock at the top of the stream and can move from rock to rock. The salmon try to progress up the stream one move at a time. If a salmon moves to a spot where the bear can move beside it in a single move, the bear will eat it. If you make it past the bear, proceed to the next station.

Station F: Locating Your Home Stream

The last step before spawning is for the remaining salmon to identify their home stream by selecting the film canister that holds the cotton ball with the correct scent. We provided

- the original film canisters and cotton balls that the salmon memorized at the beginning of the activity;
- and one canister with the scent "polluted" by another scent (to confuse the survivors).

Directions: Correctly identify the scent of your stream and you have made it back to spawn!

Wait Stations

Wait Station 1: What Does Geography Have to Do with Fish?

Use a road atlas of the Pacific Northwest to answer these questions:
Locate the Snake River. Find the length of the Snake River from Richland, Washington, to Clarkston, Washington. How many dams are located on the Snake River? Can you find a river that has more dams?

Wait Station 2: Salmon Stories

There are many books and folk tales on salmon. (See Resources for possible books.)

Directions: Select and read a book about salmon, or try to find a Native American tale about salmon.

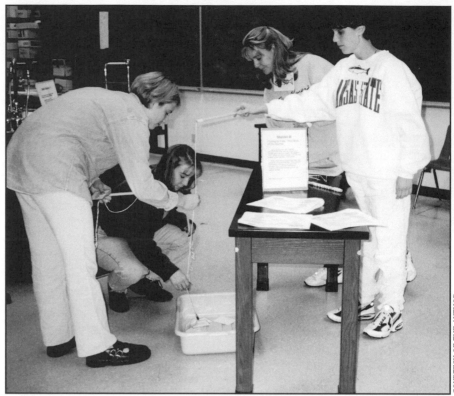

"Young salmon" fish for their fates.

The unit allowed the preservice teachers to meet three goals:
- to translate the *National Science Education Standards* (National Research Council, 1996) into investigative activities;
- to demonstrate how data collection and analysis can be incorporated into a unit integrating science and mathematics;
- and to model conceptual development in a holistic manner by merging an investigation of the life cycle of salmon with an introduction to pedagogy that uses investigative activities that begin with questions and end with the teaching of a specific science concept.

The *National Science Education Standards* were addressed on many levels. The Professional Development Standards for preservice teachers encourage inquiry into science teaching and learning through active investigation of phenomena that can be studied scientifically. Specifically, the Professional Development Standards require learning essential science content through the perspectives and methods of inquiry through active investigation that addresses issues, events, problems, or topics significant in science and of interest to participants (i.e., environmental issues) (National Research Council, 1996, p. 59).

For the Science as Inquiry Standard, this simulation required collecting and organizing data (charts of death sites, bar graphs of surviving salmon, etc.) for the purpose of analysis and interpretation. Students kept individual data on what happened to the salmon in their school, tracking and recording the mortality rates. At the conclusion of the activities, class

Figure 1. Sample Fate Cards.

Logging too close to the shoreline where you have just hatched causes erosion and silt buildup on the bottom of the stream. You unfortunately suffocate.

A kingfisher makes a meal out of you.

A great blue heron spots you and makes a grab, but you narrowly escape (this time!).

Logging has left little ground cover and the topsoil has eroded into the stream. Because of the silt buildup on the bottom of the stream, the rocks and pebbles that normally protect you as an unhatched egg are covered up and your egg is largely unprotected. You manage to hatch unscathed, but many of the other eggs were not so fortunate.

Because you are a salmon, you are hatched with a yolk sac still attached. You're called an alevin at this stage and you move slowly because of the sac. Luckily, when a hungry trout came by, you happened to be well-hidden in some rocks. The trout swims on in search of other alevin.

You manage to successfully get by the dam despite the long drop and high nitrogen content in the agitated water below. Many others were not so lucky.

A person fishing catches you, but practices catch and release. You are let go.

A bear fishing in the stream snares you with his claws, but you manage to squirm away.

Because most of the trees around your hatching location have been chopped down, the usual shade is not present, causing the stream to heat up. Fortunately, a late spring and late-melting snow keep the stream cool enough for you to survive until you are able to move farther downstream.

data regarding the number of surviving salmon and the hazards faced were compiled, charted, and graphed to draw generalizations about which hazards were most damaging to the population and which were not as damaging. We also explored the survival rate of our salmon compared to the survival rate of actual salmon populations. The activities gave students insights into "how we know what we know" and the nature of science (p. 105).

The unifying theme or fundamental concept of this activity is the Systems, Order, and Organization Content Standard: "A system is an organized group of related objects or components that form a whole." (p. 116). This simulation introduced a fundamental system in which interactions of the living (biotic) and nonliving (abiotic) components affect the survival of populations.

Other pertinent Science Content Standards related to this simulation were selected from the standards for grades K–4 and 5–8. The K–4 standards addressed include the Characteristics of Organisms, Life Cycles of

Organisms, and Organisms and Environments (p. 127). The grades 5–8 standards include Structure and Function in Living Systems, Regulation and Behavior, and Populations and Ecosystems (p. 155).

Salmon Adventures
We divided the preservice teachers into five groups, each representing a "school" of a different salmon (sockeye, chinook, coho, chum, and pink salmon). Students wore "fish tags" on their wrists or around their necks to identify themselves with a "school" and to track their activities and fate. They also received a diagram of the salmon life cycle (eggs, alevin, fry, smolt, adult, return to stream, spawning, death) as a guide.

We shared with preservice teachers that salmon return to the exact stream in which they were born to reproduce (spawn) and die. Scientists believe salmon are capable of this because they spend the first part of their lives committing the scent of their stream to memory. Out of every 100 eggs laid, only one or two salmon survive to return and spawn a new gen-

eration (Netboy, 1973).

Each "school" received a film canister that contained a uniquely scented cotton ball. We used vanilla, perfume, alcohol, cinnamon, and mouthwash. Each "young salmon" (the preservice teachers) smelled the scent and tried to commit it to memory. This simulated identification of the home stream where they must return to spawn. Once the scent was memorized, the canister was returned to the instructor and the salmon were ready to begin their journey through the activity stations.

We reminded the salmon that they would not all survive and that, if they did die, they should record where and how they died on their life cycle chart. Those who did not survive stayed with their school to observe the rest of the stations.

The activity culminated at the final station, when the few surviving salmon were challenged to once again identify the scent of their "stream" from the scented cotton balls.

A Science Springboard
In a follow-up discussion, the preservice teachers suggested some additional activities that could be conducted as part of this unit. Some of their suggestions included
- a local river study;
- the adaptation of a folk tale that describes the return of the salmon to their home stream;
- a bulletin board that depicts the salmon's journey;
- map skill instruction;
- a cooking lesson or a sample of salmon for students to taste;

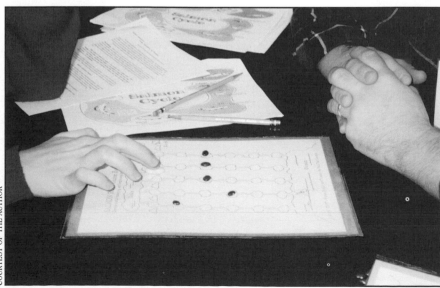

COURTESY OF THE AUTHOR

Preservice teachers play a game in which the salmon must avoid a hungry bear.

Teaching Teachers Curriculum Integration

19

- a comparison of salmon with other types of fish and their habitats or an investigation of the anatomy and systems of fish compared to other animals;
- an investigation of hydroelectric power;
- a school-based community conservation activity, such as the one described in the book *Come Back, Salmon* by Molly Cone (1992);
- a creative writing activity where students write a diary of their adventures as a salmon;
- and an art lesson based on the artifacts of the Pacific Northwest Native American people (for example, basket weaving).

The unit, the group work, and the integration of subjects had a profound effect on the preservice teachers. As they reflected on the unit in their journals, they made comments such as "I never knew this was science!" and "I only wish I had science like this when I was in school!" It was evident that these activities had put science in a whole new context for them and they felt more confident about their ability to teach science in an engaging way.

Many of the preservice teachers adapted the unit in their field experiences with elementary school children in different grade levels. From these activities, the preservice teachers easily saw how a science topic can springboard into a two- to three-week unit that uses effective science pedagogy and is reflective of the *National Science Education Standards*.

Resources

Brown, B. (1982). *Mountain in the Cloud: A Search for the Wild Salmon.* New York: Simon and Schuster.

Cone, M. (1992). *Come Back, Salmon: How a Group of Dedicated Kids Adopted Pigeon Creek and Brought It Back to Life.* San Francisco: Sierra Club Books.

Guiberson, B. (1993). *Salmon Story.* New York: Henry Holt.

National Research Council. (1996). *National Science Education Standards.* Washington, DC: National Academy Press.

Netboy, A. (1973). *The Salmon: Their Fight for Survival.* Boston: Houghton Mifflin.

Stenmark, J., Thompson, V., and Cossey, R. (1991). Salmon run (Field test version). *Family Math.* Berkeley, CA: University of California.

Werner, D. (1995). Salmon homing instinct. (Internet) Adapted from "Sniffin' Salmon" by R. Dudley, Oregon State University, and B. Hastie, Oregon Department of Education.

Also in S&C

Gannaway, S.P. (1996). Watching the watershed. *Science and Children, 33*(4), 16–18, 45.

Goethals, S. (1997). Lessons from a lake. *Science and Children, 34*(5), 32–35, 40.

Stanley, L.R. (1995). A river runs through science learning. *Science and Children, 32*(4), 12–15, 58.

M. JENICE FRENCH is an assistant professor and LAURA DOWNEY SKOCHDOPOLE is a graduate assistant, both in the Department of Elementary Education and Center for Science Education at Kansas State University in Manhattan.

Teaching Science When Your Principal Says "Teach Language Arts"

SHIRLEY V. BECKES

By Valarie L. Akerson

Interdisciplinary teaching can help teachers meet the needs of students and state and national standards.

AS AN ASSISTANT PROFESSOR OF ELEMENTARY science education, I teach many practicing teachers in graduate courses and teacher institutes. While some elementary teachers may avoid teaching science (Borko 1992; Enochs and Riggs 1990; Smith and Neale 1989), the elementary teachers who take my courses are generally very enthusiastic about teaching science and want to learn strategies to help them become better science teachers. These teachers believe that language arts are important and that science and other important disciplines can be supported by language arts, even with a reciprocal relationship (Akerson and Flanigan 2000; Dickinson, Burns, Hagen, and Locker 1997; Dickinson and Young 1998). Recently, however, several teachers have commented that principals tell them to focus on language arts and mathematics because those subject areas are being tested. While some teachers may be specifically told *not* to teach science, most are being asked only to *emphasize* language arts. This can make it difficult to satisfactorily meet state and national recommendations that indicate science content should be learned in kindergarten through high school. To help address this problem, teachers are seeking strategies that can help them focus on language arts while continuing to do a good job teaching science.

Why Use Interdisciplinary Instruction?

How do teachers respond when principals tell them to emphasize language arts? Teachers who are committed to meeting state and national standards of all curricular areas are bound to state the importance of teaching science just to help students meet those science standards. However, there are other important reasons.

First, learning science and language is reciprocal (Casteel and Isom 1994). Proponents claim that learning science can be described as a process similar to learning language, from questioning and setting a purpose to analyzing and drawing conclusions, and reporting/communicating results. Thus, processes of science and literacy learning are similar and may help the development of each discipline if the teacher is explicit in helping students note the similarities. Second, elementary students need to read, write, and communicate about something; science can provide that purpose. Finally, the most pragmatic response may be that science will soon be tested as well (in some locales it already *is* tested), using

the same high-stakes examinations that language arts and mathematics enjoy at this time. Do we really want to start at a disadvantage with science? Using an interdisciplinary strategy can help us meet those state and national science objectives in a way that supports language arts.

Connecting language arts to science makes sense because many elementary teachers' strengths are in language arts (Akerson et al. 2000; Dickinson et al. 1997). Additionally, there are similarities in national reform goals for both science and language arts. Use of language arts to promote literacy and support learning in other content areas is recommended and encouraged by the International Reading Association (IRA) and the National Council of Teachers of English (NCTE). The *Standards for the English Language Arts* recommend that language arts serve the goals of purposeful communication through reading, writing, speaking, and listening (IRA/NCTE 1996). In addition, recent reforms in science education recommend that students communicate ideas through written and oral interactions, which are applications of language arts (National Research Council 1996).

It is possible to use language arts to support science learning and to use science as a purpose for learning language arts. Interdisciplinary teaching can help teachers meet objectives for both language arts and science and still prepare our elementary students for the tests they must take.

Successful Interdisciplinary Instruction

The following suggestions offer various teacher-tested ways to include

science in a language arts curriculum. The subsections range from ideas to consider to specific strategies particularly suited for interdisciplinary science and language arts instruction.

Choose a Meaningful Theme. Elementary curricula often follow themes that do not meet both science and language arts objectives. For example, thematic instruction based on topics such as teddy bears or apples may lend itself to language arts instruction using reading and writing, but offer little to focus on with science instruction. A meaningful theme, however, promotes for discussion of big ideas and offers a greater likelihood that science objectives can also be met. For example, common themes from the *National Benchmarks for Science Literacy* (AAAS 1993)—such as systems, models, constancy and change, or scale—enable teachers and students to explore a wide variety of science concepts. Language arts skills can be incorporated in the same way as in the study of other, less scientific themes. Adams and Hamm (1998) recommend that selection of thematic big ideas meet the following criteria:

* the big idea is constant over space and time,
* the big idea broadens students' understanding of the world or what it means to be human,
* the big idea is interdisciplinary,
* the theme relates to the genuine interests of the students,
* and the interdisciplinary work lends itself to student science inquiry.

Using a *Benchmarks*-recommended theme meets those criteria.

For example, teachers in my advanced science methods course used the theme "systems" to explore such topics as electricity, seasons, chemical and physical reactions, and plant growth. Within this theme teachers learned science content as it related to interactions of components of the system, such as components of plant growth, electrical circuitry, and causes of seasonal changes.

By continually focusing teachers' attention to the theme, they were able to recognize that "systems" is a component of all science content, as recommended in the *Benchmarks*. Additionally, they were able to hone language arts skills through their oral and written discussions of the theme in class discussion and reflection paper writings.

Developing Science Skills Through Language

Explore Students' Ideas and Misconceptions. The language arts are well suited to helping teachers identify student science misconceptions. It has been long recommended that teachers of science seek to know children's ideas about a science concept prior to teaching it, so they can build on those understandings rather than teaching past the student (Driver, Guesne, and Tiberghien 1985). By using language arts skills of speaking, listening, and writing, teachers can identify students' scientific understandings.

Teachers can use class discussions to help identify children's ideas about a science topic. One useful language arts technique that lends itself to this purpose is K-W-L. Because it is more effective to identify student ideas by asking what they "think" about science content than what they "know," I've used a modified model with both elementary and adult students, such as a "T-W-L," where students tell

> *By having students write about their understandings, a teacher can track the development of student ideas from misconceptions to better understandings.*

what they *think* about the content, what else they *want* to know, and what they *learned*.

For example, in reponse to the question, "How do you think electricity works?" both children and adults shared their ideas in a large-group setting, debating their ideas while I observed their thinking on that topic. Both adults and children answered with similar incomplete conceptions prior to instruction, such as "electricity is lightning" or "electricity is power."

I used the same T-W-L technique after students (both adults and children) were asked to light a bulb using a battery and a wire. The T-W-L enabled students to express their views regarding explanations for phenomena. For the most part, both practicing teachers and elementary students tended to believe prior to experimentation that connecting a wire from one end of a battery to the bottom of a bulb would make the bulb light, but after exploring configurations, they recognized the necessity of a complete circuit. Some ideas shared after exploration included, "you need everything in a circle—that makes a circuit so the electricity can flow." Students developed oral-language skills around a shared experience, as well as developed content knowledge, something many language arts methods texts recommend (Rubin 1995; Templeton 1995; Tomkins and Hoskisson 1995; Tway 1991).

Written language can also help teachers identify students' ideas about a topic and develop profiles of individual student's thinking, particularly through science journals. For example, during a unit on sinking and floating, one elementary student's journal included the following entry, "An anchor keeps a boat floating in the river." When questioned, I found he believed the anchor did not merely hold the boat in place, but held it afloat. Following an activity involving sinkers and toy boats in a tub of water; however, the student's revised entry was, "An anchor holds a boat in place. But why does it keep floating?"

By having students write about their understandings, a teacher can track the development of student ideas from misconceptions to better understandings. The questions that students raise in their journals can also help teachers recognize areas of focus for future instruction (i.e., explore the forces that "keep boats floating").

Another benefit of using writing to elicit student thinking about science concepts is to help students develop their ideas and understand their own thinking. The *National Science Education Standards* (NRC 1996) recommends meaningful written communication of scientific understandings, which could take place in early stages of the writing process, later developing into meaningful reports of scientific investigations.

One way to develop ideas would be to have students write down observations and inferences during an investigation, such as an investigation exploring magnets. Students could record observations of magnetic items and then make written inferences for why they think certain items are magnetic and others are not. From this simple listing, students could write a formal report based on their scientific investigations of and explanations for magnetism. Students could present the reports orally or make them into books to share with classmates.

Getting the Most Out of Nonfiction Books

Share Nonfiction Literature. Nonfiction children's science literature can be used in various ways in the science classroom. First, teachers can share these books with their students during a read-aloud time (Dickinson et al. 1997). The teacher can lead discussions during and after the reading related to the scientific accuracy of what is included in the book.

For example, in *The Emperor's Egg* (Jenkins 1999) the reader is left with the idea that penguins "think" as humans do. Similarly, in *Bright Beetle* (Chrustowski 2000) the reader is left with the idea that the ladybug purposefully seeks out adventures, rather than responding to its environment as it does in nature. After reading these books, the teacher could discuss these issues with students to address

the inaccurate impressions the books present.

In addition, students can review various nonfiction books from different years, opening the discussion that different "facts" will be in books on the same subject. Students can consider why they think that is the case. Were the writers of earlier books necessarily wrong? Teachers and students can discuss the tentative nature of science, helping students understand that scientific knowledge changes with new investigations and evidence.

Another way to use nonfiction

children's literature in the science classroom is to encourage students to read such books independently. Nonfiction science books can give students background knowledge for future hands-on science investigations. Students can prepare written or oral reports to share the scientific background knowledge they have gathered from nonfiction books.

Students can also read nonfiction biographies about scientists to learn more about what scientists actually do. Reading these biographies can help students

understand scientists and perhaps help them recognize that they can become scientists, too.

Nonfiction children's literature can also help teachers develop further understandings of science content (Akerson et al. 2000). As stated earlier, elementary science teachers in particular may be less confident regarding their content knowledge. It would be virtually impossible for any teacher to have thorough understandings of all the many different science concepts. Using children's literature as a means of improving science content knowledge can be a noninti-midating way to explore scientific knowledge.

Using Available Resources

Meet Language Arts and Science Objectives. Educators recommend students experience various infor-mation sources including books, magazines, the Internet, field trips, and resource people—to meet learning objectives in both science and language arts. Students could conduct a scientific inquiry exploration—thus meeting science objectives—after researching background information in resources, which meets language arts objectives. They could meet both disciplines' objectives for meaningful communication through oral discourse regarding science content, as well as written records of their inquiry investigation.

For instance, a teacher in my class who was also taking an advanced language arts methods course conducted an investigation on factors that influence plant growth in my science methods course. From this investigation she learned under which conditions her houseplants grew best (i.e., amount of sunlight, water, and soil pH). She prepared a poster of her investigation to communicate her ideas and findings. She also wrote a formal report of her investigation in response to a language arts methods course requirement to write an informational report based on an authentic inquiry. Similar projects could be conducted with elementary students.

Include Disciplinary Instruction. While it is apparent that interdisciplinary instruction can help meet both language arts and science objectives, interdisciplinary instruction alone is not sufficient for meeting both objectives. There are times when literacy objectives can be met only through explicit literacy instruction, and science objectives can be met only through explicit science instruction.

For example, to meet science objectives, teachers cannot have students simply read, write, and share ideas about concepts. Students must also be actively engaged in inquiry investigations and experimentation. Conversely, a language arts teacher would not want to have students reading, writing, and communicating solely about science concepts. Thus, separate disciplinary instruction in both language arts and science is necessary to meet each disciplines' objectives. The goals and objectives of both science and language arts must be considered and assessed if both disciplines are appropriately addressed in elementary schools and teachers hope to help students meet both the *Standards for the English Language Arts* (IRA/NCTE 1996) and the *National Science Education Standards* (NRC 1996). Interdisciplinary instruction can help meet those objectives, but without explicit disciplinary instruction it is possible—and maybe even probable—that some disciplinary goals and objectives are lost. Teachers must balance interdisciplinary instruction with disciplinary instruction.

The Benefits

Science concepts can be explored through literacy in a fashion supported by science and literacy reforms. Although one must balance interdisciplinary with disciplinary instruction, a teacher can often concurrently help students meet both literacy and science objectives with single activities, such as *Benchmarks* (AAAS 1993) and *Standards* (IRA/NCTE 1993) communications objectives with written and oral descriptions of science inquiries. With thoughtful interdisciplinary instruction, teachers will be able to continue to teach science successfully without compromising literacy instruction.

Valarie L. Akerson is an assistant professor of science education at Washington State University in Richland.

Resources

Akerson, V.L., and J. Flanigan. 2000. Preparing preservice teachers to use an interdisciplinary approach to science and language arts instruction. *Journal of Science Teacher Education, 11*(4), 287–313.

Akerson, V.L., L.B. Flick, and N.G. Lederman. 2000. Influence of primary children's ideas in science on teaching practice. *Journal of Research in Science Teaching, 37*(4), 363–385.

American Association for the Advancement of Science. 1993. *Benchmarks for Science Literacy.* New York: Oxford.

Borko, H. 1993. The integration of content and pedagogy in teaching. In *Critical Issues in Reforming Elementary Teacher Preparation in Mathematics and Science Conference Proceedings.* Edited by A.L. Gardner and K.F. Cochran. Greeley, Colo.: University of Northern Colorado.

Casteel, C.P., and B.A. Isom. 1994. Reciprocal processes in science and literacy learning. *The Reading Teacher, 47*(7), 538–545.

Chrustowski, R. 2000. *Bright Beetle.* Canada: Henry Holt.

Dickinson, V.L., J. Burns, E. Hagen, and K. Locker. 1997. Becoming better primary science teachers: A description of our journey. *Journal of Science Teacher Education, 8*(4), 295–311.

Dickinson, V.L., and T.A. Young. 1998. Elementary science and language arts: Should we blur the boundaries? *School Science and Mathematics, 98,* 334–339.

Driver, R., E. Guesne, and A. Tiberghien. 1985. *Children's Ideas in Science.* Milton Keynes: Open University.

Enochs, L.G., and I.M. Riggs. 1990. Further development of an elementary science teaching efficacy belief scale instrument: A preservice elementary scale. *School Science and Mathematics, 90*(6), 694–706.

Fulwiler, T. 1987. *Teaching with Writing.* Portsmouth, N.H.: Boynton-Cook.

International Reading Association and National Council of Teachers of English. 1996. *Standards for the English Language Arts.* Newark, Del.: Author.

Jenkins, M. 1999. *The Emperor's Egg.* Cambridge, Mass.: Candlewick.

National Research Council. 1996. *National Science Education Standards.* Alexandria, Va.: National Academy.

Ogle, D.M. 1986. K-W-L: A teaching model that develops active reading of expository text. *The Reading Teacher, 39*(6), 564–570.

Pappas, C.C., B.Z. Kiefer, and L.S. Levstik. 1995. *An Integrated Language Perspective in the Elementary School: Theory into Action.* White Plains, N.Y.: Longman.

Rubin, D. 1995. *Teaching Elementary Language Arts: An Integrated Approach.* 5th ed. Boston: Allyn and Bacon.

Smith, D.C., and D.C. Neale. 1989. The construction of subject matter knowledge in primary science teaching. *Teaching and Teacher Education, 5*(1), 1–20.

Templeton, S. 1995. *Children's Literacy: Contexts for Meaningful Learning.* Boston: Houghton Mifflin.

Tompkins, G.E., and K. Hoskisson. 1995. *Language Arts: Content and Teaching Strategies.* 3rd ed. Englewood Cliffs, N.J.: Merrill.

Tway, E. 1991. The elementary classroom. In *Handbook of Research on Teaching the English Language Arts.* Edited by J. Flood, J.M. Jensen, D. Lapp, and J.R. Squire. New York: Macmillan.

Assessment for Preservice Teachers

By Jeffrey R. Lehman

Recent reforms in science education have called for science instruction that involves higher-order thinking skills, cooperative group work, physical and mental student involvement, and interdisciplinary learning. But as curricula and instruction change to reflect these diversified goals, forms of assessment must also change so that teachers are able to evaluate accurately their students' progress.

The assessment techniques described in this article reflect the recent reforms in science instruction. For each type of assessment, I've included objectives, a description of the technique, and criteria for meeting the objectives. I've used these techniques effectively with preservice elementary science methods students both to evaluate their progress and to model types of assessment they might eventually use with their students.

Anecdotal Observations

Objective: This method fosters students' involvement in class activities through written feedback concerning their participation.

Description: During each class investigation in which students work in groups, randomly select a few students and observe their behavior. Record your anecdotal observations on a class activity comment form (see Figure 1) which will be given to students at the end of the class. Each student may receive as many as five comment forms per semester.

Criteria: Periodic observations throughout the semester yield data that are used to assess the extent of students' group participation.

Performance Assessment

Objectives: Students will demonstrate the appropriate use of measuring devices typically used in elementary science; they will apply science concepts and skills by completing a hands-on science activity; and they will collect data and draw appropriate conclusions from that data.

Description: Students individually complete various tasks at performance-assessment tables. For example, you might ask students to determine the mass of a block of wood. At the table, students would find a balance, spring scale, metric ruler, and graduated cylinders. The students would then need to select the appropriate tool and use it properly to complete the task. Or, you might ask students to build a circuit with a switch, two cells in series, and two lamps in parallel; draw a diagram of the setup; and show the completed circuit to you.

Criteria: Students are evaluated on the accuracy of their responses.

Reflective Journal

Objectives: Students will connect topics from elementary science methods to prior coursework and theory. They also will elaborate upon class activities by suggesting ways to extend, modify, and/or integrate them into other subject areas. Finally, students will carry on a professional dialogue concerning issues related to science education.

Description: Students keep a daily log of reactions to each class session. Have students use their journals to focus on areas that need further explanation, new concepts learned through the activity, and "what if" questions. Collect the journals at least four times during the semester. In this way, you can establish a professional dialogue with your students in a confidential atmosphere.

Reflective journals can reveal students' prior misconceptions in science and can suggest topics to incorporate into future lessons. For example, one student wrote that she "never realized the mixing of color pigments was different from the mixing of colored lights." Another mentioned that she still had difficulty using a concrete model to explain the phases of the moon, thus suggesting that additional instruction on this point would be warranted. Another student related our lessons on magnetism and the use of a cow magnet to a recent article she had read concerning iron in cereal.

Many students have never kept a science journal and are skeptical as to how it can be used in the subject; by the end of the semester, however, just as many students say that they will miss writing about science ideas, questions, and concepts.

Criteria: Provide written feedback to students each time the journals are collected. At the end of the semester, assign a rating (good, average, or poor) based upon the number of entries and the quality of reflection.

Figure 1. Anecdotal observations of students in the classroom can be recorded by teachers on a simple form and given to students after that class period.

Student:	Jane Smith
Activity:	Color
Date:	October 24, 1994
Observer:	Dr. Parr

Comments: When you were observing the colors in the comic strips, you used the hand lens properly — much improvement from last time. I noticed that you did not have much to say to your group members during the activity. Be sure to offer your explanations and to question your partners concerning any aspects of the activity that you are unsure of.

Reflective Problem Solving

Objectives: Students will solve problems using common manipulatives and consider the scientific reasoning behind their attempted solutions. Students will then create problems for children or their peers to solve, and they will diagnose strategies and identify misconceptions.

Description: In addition to writing in daily logs, have students write about their thought processes as they attempt to solve problems. For example, show students an egg floating in the middle of a liquid-filled glass and ask them to reproduce the setup. Then, have them give a written explanation of why they attempted various solutions. As in the reflective journal, these written descriptions can reveal student misconceptions.

After solving a number of instructor-assigned problems, have each student create three problem situations for either their peers or elementary-age children to solve (remind them to consider safety precautions while creating the problem situations). Students must ask the problem solvers to explain the reasoning behind their attempted solutions and cue them when they exhaust their ideas. Any science misconceptions they might have would be identified during these times of explanation.

Criteria: On instructor-assigned problems, students are assessed on the amount of detail they record concerning their strategies and reasoning. Written reactions to problems used with children or peers must include evidence that the methods student probed problem solvers for reasons behind attempted solutions, asked for explanations, and identified any content inaccuracies in those explanations.

Dealing with Data

Objectives: Students will engage in integrated mathematics and science lessons and identify both mathematics and science skills and concepts contained within each lesson.

Description: Give each student five bags of M&M™ candies. Students should empty the bags, collect data relating to the candies, and then organize and interpret the data.

For example, students could determine the range or average number of candies per bag. Or, they could record the number of candies of each color in each bag, noting the most common color. They then might organize the data into a table or a graph and begin to look for patterns (see Figure 2).

Criteria: On a written examination, students either must create an outline of an integrated mathematics/science lesson or identify the mathematics and science concepts and skills contained within a suggested scenario. Students are assessed on the quality and accuracy of their answers.

Cooperative Learning Model

Objectives: Students will model cooperative learning behavior and demonstrate appropriate elementary science teaching techniques to a small group of peers.

Description: Divide the class into cooperative groups of four, and assign each group member a different topic within the same theme on which to become an expert (for example, if the class is studying simple machines, students in each group may be assigned an aspect of the topic of lever, inclined plane, pulley, or friction). Give students a week to research their topics individually, then ask all classmates studying the same topic to meet and discuss their findings.

Figure 2. When data are organized, patterns may become evident. This chart presents data students gathered during the M&Ms sorting exercise.

Sample Number	Red	Orange	Green	Yellow	Tan	Brown
1	8	1	12	15	9	12
2	12	4	4	17	6	14
3	8	10	5	5	12	17
4	7	4	2	1	6	23
5	4	3	9	7	10	12

Methods students should use this time to clarify ideas, ask the instructor questions, and explain to their classmates how they are going to teach the topic to the other members of their group.

In the next class period, have students meet in their cooperative groups of four and ask each one to teach a 20-minute lesson to their peers. If possible, videotape these lessons for later analysis.

Criteria: The methods students' lessons are assessed on the basis of a peer-evaluation form filled out by each group member. In addition, the instructor views a videotape of the students' presentation and judges the appropriateness of teaching strategies as well as the accuracy of content. The experience of seeing themselves teach on videotape is most helpful to those students who have never before had that opportunity.

Group Exam Question

Objectives: Students will discuss an exam question as a group and then decide whether or not to incorporate other group members' suggestions into their individual answers.

Description: For example, you might give each group of four students a double-pan balance and two bags of 10 pennies, one labeled "A" and holding pennies minted prior to 1982, and the other labeled "B" and holding pennies minted after 1982. Then ask students to make one *quantitative* observation concerning the pennies in bag A and one *qualitative* observation about the pennies in bag B, to determine the relative masses of the two groups of 10 pennies, and then to explain why the two groups had different masses. At the end of the investigation, each student must submit answers to the questions using the information gleaned from the group or by providing an answer on his or her own.

Most students have never participated in a group activity during an examination. Frequently, students have told me that having the group investigation at the start of the test makes them less anxious when they proceed to the written portion.

Criteria: Students are assessed on the basis of the accuracy of their responses.

Summing Up

At the end of the semester, students will have experienced a number of different assessment techniques. In my class, I pool the data collected from these various assessments and assign values to them to determine each student's grade for the course.

At the end of the semester, I've heard many preservice teachers say that they plan to use the assessment techniques modeled in our classroom when they begin teaching elementary school science; later, I have observed them doing so. As educators continue to restructure their science programs to reflect diversified science instruction, assessment techniques must be continually refined to produce valid and reliable assessment.

Resources

American Association for the Advancement of Science. (1989). *Project 2061: Science for all Americans.* Washington, DC: Author.

Hassard, J. (1990). Science experiences: *Cooperative learning and the teaching of science.* Menlo Park, CA: Addison-Wesley.

Lehman, J.R. (1992). Preservice problem solving. *Science and Children, 29*(4), 30-31.

Mathematical Science Education Board. (1993). *Measuring up: Prototypes for mathematical assessment.* Washington, DC: National Academy Press.

National Council of Teachers of Mathematics. (1989). *Curriculum and evaluation standards for school mathematics.* Reston, VA: Author.

National Science Teachers Association. (1992). *Scope, sequence, and coordination of secondary school science.* Washington, DC: Author.

Stenmark, J.K. (Ed.). (1991). *Mathematics assessment: Myths, models, good questions, and practical suggestions.* Reston, VA: National Council of Teachers of Mathematics.

JEFFREY R. LEHMAN is an associate professor of science education at Slippery Rock (Pennsylvania) University.

Standards Direct Preservice Teacher Portfolios

By Christine Moseley

The ability to think about what one does and why—assessing past actions, current situations, and intended outcomes—is vital to intelligent practice, practice that is reflective rather than routine. As the time in the teaching process when teachers stop to think about their work and make sense of it, reflection influences how one grows as a professional by influencing how successfully one is able to learn from one's experiences (Richert, 1990, p. 525).

The need for teachers to be reflective practitioners has been well established since the National Commission on Excellence in Education (1983) recommended that teachers become active decision makers concerning all elements of teaching and learning. Teachers must not only know the subject matter but also have the ability to understand it from the perspective of the learner.

When preservice teachers analyze and reflect on lesson plans and instructional practices, they gain insight into effective teaching, thereby making appropriate decisions for learners and themselves. Portfolios provide an opportunity and a structure for teachers to document and describe their teaching; articulate their professional knowledge; and reflect on what, how, and why they teach. Structured teaching portfolios promote reflection among both preservice and experienced teachers.

Two years ago, I became committed to sharing the *National Science Education Standards* (National Research Council, 1996) with the preservice teachers in my class. My challenge was incorporating the *Standards* into an already full science methods course. A required portfolio became the most logical answer. With the portfolio organized around the *Standards,* my students not only have practice in reflection techniques but also are gaining an understanding of the *Standards* and how the *Standards* can be implemented into daily lessons and teaching strategies.

Purpose of the Science Portfolio

The science methods course portfolio is an edited collection of evidence of professional growth and reflections representing progress toward preservice teachers' personal goals, the national science teaching standards, and Oklahoma State University's Core Concept of Integration. The portfolio also provides the basis for self-assessment and instructor evaluation of the preservice teacher's progress.

Personal Goals. Each preservice teacher is required to list and describe a minimum of five personal, professional goals. These goals help students focus on their future professional plans and the steps required to achieve those plans. Students are also asked to imagine and describe their ideal teaching position five years after graduation. Then they are to consider the following questions:

- What will you need to know to perform well in that position?

Suggestions for Content

Standards	Suggested Evidence
Teaching Standard A: Teachers of science plan an inquiry-based science program for their students.	Unit/lesson plans Learning centers Interactive bulletin boards Samples of student work Field trips
Teaching Standard B: Teachers of science guide and facilitate learning.	Lesson plans with modifications Teaching styles Videotape of teaching Case studies Multicultural lesson plans Activity centers
Teaching Standard C: Teachers of science engage in ongoing assessment of their teaching and of student learning.	Self-made tests Philosophy of education Resume Transcripts Future plans/goals Alternative assessment ideas Pre-assessment products Tutoring assessment
Teaching Standard D: Teachers of science design and manage learning environments that provide students with the time, space, and resources needed for learning science.	Diagram of classroom Parental involvement plan Discipline plan Substitute experience Personal library resources Classroom safety plan Classroom science materials list Use of technology plan List of community resources Local field trips Outdoor education lessons
Teaching Standard E: Teachers of science develop communities of science learners that reflect the intellectual rigor of scientific inquiry and the attitudes and social values conducive to science learning.	Articles written Grants/awards Workshops/conferences attended Computer literacy sample Work experience Group projects Science fair projects Research papers
Teaching Standard F: Teachers of science actively participate in the ongoing planning and development of the school science program.	Community service Professional organization member College organizations Leadership roles Interviews with teachers and principals Teacher inservice

- What skills will you need?
- What attitudes and dispositions will you need to develop to succeed and be satisfied with your work?
- What experiences do you need to prepare for this position?

Throughout the portfolio, students complete a "Brief Reflection Form" (See Figure 1) for each piece of evidence (specific items such as reports and work samples that document outcomes) in each section, explaining how the evidence represents progress toward their goals (see Suggestions for Content).

National Science Teaching Standards. "To teach science as portrayed by the *Standards*, teachers must have theoretical and practical knowledge and abilities about science, learning, and science teaching" (*National Science Education Standards*, 1996, p. 28). To assure that competency and understanding of each of the six teaching standards have been met by the preservice teacher, the portfolio must include a minimum of three pieces of evidence for each standard. The evidence and accompanying reflections in the portfolio show how knowledge and skills in these standards have been acquired (see Suggestions for Content).

The "Brief Reflection Form" that accompanies each item of evidence explains how the preservice teacher is making progress toward gaining competency in one or more of the standards.

Portfolio Requirements

A true portfolio must be student owned. The actual content should reflect what each student knows, cares about, and is able to do. Preservice teachers are given explicit directions

Preservice Teacher Portfolio Samples

Teaching Standard A: Teachers of science plan an inquiry-based science program for their students.

One student included in her portfolio a traditional science lesson taken from a 1988 science textbook. She transformed this into a new lesson following the outline of the learning cycle. She wrote, "I learned that writing a lesson plan is much more involved now than it was when I went through teacher education 25 years ago. I also learned that writing a complete lesson plan now allows you to answer a lot of your own questions about a concept. The learning cycle actively involves the student and teacher as partners in the learning process."

Teaching Standard B: Teachers of science guide and facilitate learning.

"Body features" learning center. "I wanted to create an activity that kids could do themselves, with a minimum amount of help from the teacher. My third-grade son's teacher was willing to allow me to use her students as guinea pigs since they had recently finished a unit on the human body."

Graph transformations. "This is the first time I have given my students the opportunity to work collaboratively in class on a lesson that I have not already presented. They had graphing skills. They were to use those skills to graph the functions and observe the change in the graph that was caused by a corresponding change I made in the basic equation. This item represents my commitment to allowing my students to construct their own knowledge from what they already should know."

Teaching Standard C: Teachers of science engage in ongoing assessment of their teaching and of student learning.

Reflective journal of own teaching. "It was very time consuming! I became aware of just how much thought I put into what I am going to do, what I have done, and what I should have done."

Teaching Standard D: Teachers of science design and manage learning environments that provide students with the time, space, and resources needed for learning science.

Parental involvement plan. "These items are evidence of my goals, both as a parent and as a teacher. As a parent I want to be involved in my children's education, and I want to feel that the teachers and administrators want me to be involved. That attitude would dictate my actions as a teacher so that I would be sure to keep parents informed about what's going on in my classroom and what opportunities they have to become involved."

Teaching Standard E: Teachers of science develop communities of science learners that reflect the intellectual rigor of scientific inquiry and the attitudes and social values conducive to science learning.

Web page. "One of my personal goals is to force myself to get over my awe of computers because I don't want my students to be computer-phobic. I had seen Web sites that contain mathematics content material and of course had used the Internet for research and browsing, but I had no idea of what was involved in producing those Web pages. I felt proud of myself that I stayed with it even when I reached the point of frustration."

Teaching Standard F: Teachers of science actively participate in the ongoing planning and development of the school science program.

Web page. "I had created my Web page, but only my students had used it. With Teaching Standard F in mind, I decided to make the information about the Web page available to other faculty. This was a big step for me to publicize my Web page and leave it and myself open for evaluation."

Parents as teachers. "My younger son's teacher invites parents of her students to come into the classroom under the heading of 'parents as teachers.'" I decided to try out the cohesion/adhesion lesson. They were really impressed with the 'cat's meow' activity."

---

about the form and procedure of portfolio documentation, as well as guidelines about the types and amount of evidence to include and about the method of evaluation; however, they make personal decisions regarding the particular evidence selected to satisfy the purpose of the portfolio. While the individual preservice teacher determines the exact nature of the portfolio contents, the following items are required in the portfolio (a three-ring binder with divided sections):

- a title page and table of contents;
- a minimum of five personal, professional goals;
- a minimum of three items of evidence for each national science teaching standard;
- a one-page "Brief Reflection Form" for each item of evidence;
- a reflective commentary (see Figure 2);
- and one professional journal article critique for each national science teaching standard.

Portfolio Assessment

To assess the science portfolios, I use two types of rubrics: analytical and holistic (See Figure 3). The analytical rubric consists of criteria that are subdivided into different levels of performance. This rubric allows me to look in-depth at individual components of the portfolio and offer suggestions and comments.

Performance on the individual components helps me determine the holistic grade that best describes the overall quality of the portfolio.

Final Thoughts

I have found that using portfolios in this way is critical in influencing preservice teachers' beliefs and attitudes toward becoming reflective practitioners. Furthermore, using the national science teaching standards as the basis for the portfolios positively influenced the elementary education students' self-concepts about their ability to teach.

Semester after semester I hear comments such as "I actually know more about science than I thought I did" and "I think I am ready to teach science now!"

By making the *Standards* the basis for the science portfolio, my students are experiencing the integration of the complex nature of science education and personalizing it into their own philosophies of teaching. Once the portfolios are completed, the students have gained an understanding of what the *Standards* mean and have gathered personal evidence that demonstrates their competency in those standards. They actually feel good about science and their ability to teach it.

Christine Moseley is an assistant professor of science education at Oklahoma State University in Stillwater.

Resources

National Research Council. (1996). *National Science Education Standards*. Washington, DC: National Academy Press.

Richert, A.E. (1990). Teaching teachers to reflect: A consideration of program structure. *Journal of Curriculum Studies, 22*(6), 509–527.

The National Commission on Excellence in Education. (1993). *A Nation at Risk: The Imperative for Educational Reform*. Washington, DC: Author.

FIGURE 3. Science portfolio assessment.

Analytical Evaluation

3=Superb
2=Proficient
1=Weak

A. Professional Goals
3 Articulate, represented depth and breadth as professional, clear and precise, unique.
2 Adequate, represented essential competencies as professional, coherent.
1 Further expansion and articulation needed.
Comments

B. Organizational Requirements
3 Used many different levels of creativity to meet requirements. Showed the highest level of organization. Reader friendly. Table of contents thorough, complete. Categories well defined in professional appearance, logical sequence evident.
2 Met basic requirements. Showed a moderate amount of organization.
1 Did not meet basic requirements, incomplete and without organization. Lacked qualities of professionalism.
Comments

C. Evidence
3 Contained all pieces of evidence. Thoroughly related to personal goals and science standards. Congruent with organization, diverse, represents depth and breadth, documents professional growth and change, absence of unfocused or redundant evidence.

C. Evidence *(continued)*
2 Contained most pieces of required evidence. Evidence was adequately linked to personal goals and standards. Demonstration of competence, absence of unfocused or redundant evidence.
1 Lacked all or some evidence. Evidence had no connection to personal goals and/or standards. Purposes unclear, lacked professional appearance.
Comments

D. Reflections of evidence
3 Evidence related to goals and standards. Answered questions accurately and completely. Typed, easy to read. Reflected an understanding of assignment. Descriptive, clear, and explicit. Documented attainment of specific goals. Professional appearance.
2 Identified evidence; set purpose for inclusion; explanatory; professional appearance.
1 Purpose of evidence unclear; more elaboration needed; required inference by reader.
Comments

E. Reflective commentary
3 Articulate; demonstrated self-analysis and self-evaluation; emphasis on process; growth evident.
2 Coherent; some evidence of self-discussion; emphasis on process.
1 Reporting rather than self-discussion; unfocused.
Comments

Holistic Evaluation

3 Well organized; creative; displayed a high degree of effort and care; cohesive; well-chosen evidence with well-written reflections; articulate and interesting; displayed the highest level of insight, organization, and professionalism; met all requirements; showed high level of evidence of understanding and proficiency of science teaching standards; contained a variety of teaching materials and strategies; articles chosen from technical sources; exciting to look through; work reflected enthusiasm for science and teaching.

2 Loosely organized; minimum creativity; only required amount of effort given; less obvious evidence with less careful reflection; met most of the requirements; displayed an average level of insight, organization, and professionalism; reflections included but not always explanatory; showed some evidence of an understanding and proficiency of science teaching standards; contained some variety of evidence; factors most likely to be missing were indications of student enthusiasm, self-assessment, extensive investigations, and analysis of information.

1 Included almost no creative work and consisted mainly of pages copied from a textbook or journal; not organized, sloppy; very little or no insight into the development; incomplete; did not meet requirements; evidence was not adequate for each standard; reflections were not clear; little variety of evidence; did not reflect the author's personal goals; showed little evidence of understanding and proficiency of the science teaching standards; no technical articles critiqued.

Using Effective Demonstrations for Motivation

By Michael P. Freedman

Simple suggestions for classroom demonstrations

As an elementary educator you have probably seen a thousand versions of "show and tell," the classic activity of students communicating their ideas as they describe favorite objects or share a memento from a recent experience. But, have you ever considered how "show and tell" could apply to the science classroom? In the same way that children express their ideas in "show and tell," science demonstrations can provide teachers with opportunities to "show" science phenomena and "tell" students about their underlying principles. Demonstrations, when used in the elementary classroom, are an avenue to motivate students to do their own experimenting.

Demonstrations and discrepant events—events that produce an unexpected outcome—capture students' attention and enable teachers to introduce or explain a science concept in a highly visual or auditory way. In addition, these events prompt students' curiosity and develop both their critical-thinking and problem-solving skills. I've incorporated teaching the best practices of effective demonstrations in the graduate course, "Science: Learning and Teaching in the Early Childhood and Elementary Grades." This article addresses some of the issues involved in conducting safe, educational, and entertaining demonstrations in the science classroom; this will stimulate elementary students to learn from these presentations and then demonstrate their own experiments.

Creating a Good "Show"

In the graduate course students select a demonstration or discrepant event and give a five- to seven-minute presentation of it. At the first class session, I randomly assign each student a performance date evenly distributed throughout the duration of the course.

To begin, I emphasize that a demonstration or the presentation of a discrepant event is a teacher-centered performance in front of an audience of students to be used as a motivator or a direct teaching strategy. Many preservice teachers confuse the notion of a demonstration with that of a hands-on experiment, which is a student-centered experience that enables a child to investigate science phenomena and to discover science concepts, principles, and laws. Teachers expect students to be motivated to learn and develop their own experiments by using these introductory demonstrations.

I explain that I will be modeling a few successful demonstrations to help preservice teachers learn how to conduct future demonstrations to motivate their students. The demonstrations I conduct include such activities as creating a simple doll figure from items hidden in my pockets to illustrate the ideas of center of gravity and

CLEO PHOTOGRAPHY

Successful demonstrations can motivate children to explore science principles and conduct their own investigations.

equilibrium; attracting an empty aluminum soft-drink can to a balloon secretly charged by friction to explore electrostatics; and working with liquid soap, ground pepper, and water to explore surface tension. One of my favorite discrepant events is placing cans of one brand of diet and regular cola in water and observing students' reactions as one sinks and the other floats. Modeling the demonstrations helps the preservice teachers learn that successful demonstrations include several elements.

Purpose. Every good demonstration or discrepant event has a purpose. The purpose is related to a particular science concept that forms the basis of a learning outcome. For example, if students are learning about what constitutes a chemical reaction, a teacher might conduct a demonstration using baking soda and vinegar in a clear plastic bottle. The dramatic reaction when these substances

meet in the bottle provides students with a visual example of one of the indications that a chemical reaction has occurred (production of a gas). Following this introductory experience, students can conduct further studies on the topic.

Planning. Good demonstrations reflect the importance of planning in the science classroom. On the day I model the demonstrations, students observe that the materials and equipment have been set up prior to class. This shows them some of the planning that was required to prepare for the event. The setup should be arranged on a convenient-sized surface and located for optimal viewing for all students. When using multiple demonstrations of the same concept, sequence the demonstrations by increasing difficulty. Throughout the modeling of a demonstration, I emphasize the value of practice. Prior rehearsal permits a smooth perfor-

mance, instills confidence in the teacher, and provides a valid estimate of the time to complete the demonstration and timing of the events in it.

Repeatability. An event or phenomenon can occur very quickly, so another important attribute of an effective demonstration is its repeatability.

Simplicity and Safety. Most successful demonstrations and discrepant events use familiar, safe, and simple materials. Plastic-ware, newspaper, polyethylene bags, string, rubber bands, and other household items are the mainstays of many effective elementary demonstrations. The polyethylene bag that protects my daily newspaper offers an innovative alternative to the commonly seen demonstration of using a knitting needle to pierce a balloon. Filling the bag with water and piercing it with a few sharpened pencils is a simple and easy way to show that spaces exist in polymer structures.

Regarding safety issues when demonstrating, I encourage preservice teachers to exhibit the same precautions that they exemplify when conducting hands-on activities with students. Some of my suggestions include using plastic or nonshatter containers, batteries instead of electrical outlets, small quantities of household chemicals, protective clothing (including gloves), and goggles.

Visibility and Showmanship. Another important factor in the success of a demonstration is visibility, or making sure that students can see what is happening and what materials are being used. Whenever possible, I use large objects and clear transparent containers to increase visibility of the demonstration. For example, a good-size balloon that will hold sufficient charge to attract an aluminum soft-drink can is clearly visible, and a

FIGURE 1. Evaluation rubric.

Each of the attributes listed below will be scored on a scale of one to ten. The overall grade for the demonstration performance is an average of the five scores.

Clarity of concept _____
    The concept is understood by teacher and clear to class members.

Teaching _____
    The concept is taught to the class, including inquiry and questions.
    Adequate wait time is allowed.

Visual Presentation _____
    Students in the class can see the details of the demonstration.
    Teacher faces and engages the class.
    Objects are large enough to be seen clearly.

Interest _____
    The demonstration captures the attention and imagination of the class.

Evidence of Research _____
    Some choose the "easiest"; others search for more depth, inquiry, relation to principles of science, and multiple demonstrations of the same principle or concept.

Comments:

Overall Grade (Average of components) _____

2 L plastic bottle makes my homemade Cartesian diver easy to see.

Variations in room lighting, effective backgrounds, and the location of the demonstration in the classroom can also enhance visibility. I use white or light-colored backgrounds to show events or objects through clear containers, and I avoid having windows or chalkboards at my back. Circular or semicircular classroom seating arrangements allow for excellent visibility for demonstrations. When appropriate, I move about the classroom to present students with a closer view of the demonstration. I also use the overhead projector to enhance visibility. For example, if I place a clear shallow plastic dish containing water sprinkled with ground black pepper on an overhead projector, an entire class can view the effect of a drop of liquid soap on the surface tension of the water.

In addition to visibility, showmanship can also enhance a demonstration. Just as a theater performer focuses on the audience, I advise preservice teachers to use all facets of their personality to make a demonstration more effective. Be an actor on stage! Use humor and vary voice levels; maintain a steady banter; continually question students; and comment on what, where, and when to watch. A teacher might incorporate suspense by pulling items from pockets, out of boxes, or from other hiding places.

First the Show, Now the "Tell"

Once preservice students understand the elements of a successful demonstration or "show," they are ready to learn more about the "tell," or the part of the demonstration that explores the science behind the phenomenon observed. Explain to the class that if the purpose of the demonstration or discrepant event is to initiate inquiry, then as teachers they are to "tell" their future students as little as possible. Instead, the teacher should encourage his or her students to report what they have observed and speculate on how the event works. The yearning for explanation forms the rationale for the inquiry-based learning that will follow. Consider students' surprise at seeing one can of soda float and another sink. Why does this happen? Students are typically eager to investigate what makes the cans different. One such investigation might involve measuring and comparing the masses of the can, leading to the discovery that one can is denser (contains more sugar) than the other, thus explaining why it sinks.

If the purpose of the demonstration is to illustrate a specific concept, then teachers can question students to elicit observations, probe for explanations, and come to closure with generalizations leading to an understanding and an ownership of the concept. It is the teacher's job to encourage children to "tell" what they've learned from the demonstration through this process.

If one must "tell" the concept behind the demonstration, he or she should do so at the end, after students have had a chance to share their ideas. "Tell" to make sure the concept is clearly verbalized or stated for all to hear. "Tell" to review or to summarize. "Tell" to foster closure for best understanding.

Assessing the Demonstrations

After discussing ideas about effective demonstrations, preservice teachers are usually eager to conduct demonstrations on their own. To assess students' performances, I follow a simple rubric presented to the students at the same time the assignment is given (see Figure 1). The rubric evaluates the performance based upon established attributes of a demonstration. By giving this form to the preservice teachers early on, everyone is clear about the learning outcomes associated with the assignment and the criteria that assess these outcomes. The rubric fosters consistency of evaluation across all performances and enables students to accept the validity of their evaluation.

Many of the demonstrations that preservice teachers conduct are not new or original—designing and creating effective science demonstrations is a difficult task even for brilliant scientists. For this assignment I encourage students to consult resources for ideas and well-tested, "guaranteed-to-be-successful" demonstrations. These resources include journals, school- and district-developed curriculum materials, and textbook publisher support packets for teachers, books of science demonstrations and activities, as well as Internet sites devoted to elementary science teaching and learning. These tried-and-true demonstrations, though well worn to us, are novel and exciting to a new audience. By the end of the course, most students feel that demonstrations are a highly interesting, motivating way to begin a lesson. Students have experienced firsthand the enthusiasm and energy generated by a demonstration and have seen how the demonstration's spark can carry over to other science activities.

Resources

Brown, J. (1984). *333 More Science and Experiments*. Blue Ridge Summit, PA: Tab Books.
Herbert, D. (1983). *Mr. Wizard's 400 Experiments in Science*. North Bergen, NJ: Book Lab.
Liem, T.L. (1987). *Invitations to Science Inquiry (2nd Ed.)*. Chino Hills, CA: Science Inquiry Enterprises.
Summerlin, L.R., and Ealy, J. (1985). *Chemical Demonstrations: A Sourcebook for Teachers*. Washington, DC: American Chemical Society.

Internet

Bill Nye the Science Guy
  http://www.billnye.com
Dr. Bob's Interesting Science Stuff
  http://www.frontiernet.net/~docbob/
Science Is Fun
  http://www.scifun.chem.wisc.edu
The Teaching Tank
  http://www.tchg.com/

Also in S&C

Jeffries, C. (1999). Activity selection: It's more than the fun factor. *Science and Children, 37*(8), 26–29, 63.
Jeran, C. (1999). Exploring experimental design. *Science and Children, 36*(4), 24–27, 60.

Michael P. Freedman is assistant professor of curriculum and teaching at Fordham University Graduate School of Education in New York City.

Managing Hands-on Inquiry

By Alan D. Rossman

In the past decade, we've seen hundreds of reports that call for sweeping changes in the ways and means of science education. Many of these reports call for a shift away from conventional teaching in favor of methods that actively involve students in hands-on, inquiry experiences. These methods, centered on student investigation and problem solving, cultivate positive attitudes toward science and learning in general.

A New Approach

We know that adopting hands-on, inquiry-based methods can bring great rewards. Teachers who use these methods successfully are almost guaranteed higher student enthusiasm and involvement, and deeper understanding of content and concepts. In addition, the autonomy students experience enables them to learn to think for themselves, both critically and creatively.

A recent, informal survey conducted by the Chicago Botanic Garden revealed an interesting and relevant paradox. The respondents (elementary teachers from Chicago's public schools) devoted only about 10 percent of their science-teaching time to the inquiry approach, yet 100 percent of these same teachers agreed that hands-on inquiry is the best way to teach science. Why, then, if teachers are so convinced of the benefits of inquiry teaching methods, are they reluctant to use them?

Understanding the Risks

Many teachers perceive hands-on inquiry methods as more "risky" than conventional teaching methods. They are often daunted by the possibility that "things could go wrong." It is true that as students manipulate science materials and inquire on their own, the element of risk increases. Yet these risks are manageable and

should not prevent teachers from adopting an inquiry approach.

Navigating the risks means accepting a change in the relationship between teacher and learner. In contrast to conventional, didactic forms of teaching, hands-on inquiry redistributes the responsibility for learning to students and increases the importance of their interaction with materials. As the teacher's role changes from that of presenter to guide (facilitator), the role of the student changes from passive recipient of information to participant in the creation of understanding. Under these conditions, there is a fundamental shift from an emphasis on teaching to an emphasis on learning. From these shifting roles and the transfer of responsibility emerges the need for a different approach to classroom management.

Managing the Risks

Effectively managing the hands-on, inquiry classroom can mean the difference between chaos and real learning. In order to break down the barriers and reduce instructional risks, the following guidelines should be considered before, during, and after hands-on inquiry:

- *Plan and prepare.* Inquiry lessons need to be planned carefully. In order for students to take a more active and independent role in learning, your instructions must be clear. Planning will also help you use the available time most efficiently. Prepare and organize all materials before class begins. Pretest activities and materials so that you can anticipate and address difficulties and possible sources of confusion.

- **Create problem intrigue.** Problems to solve and questions to investigate are at the heart of inquiry. The problem should captivate students' attention, be meaningful, and allow a wide range of individual responses. It should also serve to enliven, extend, and reinforce the content under study. There will never be a shortage of suitable problems—just listen to students' questions and go from there!

- **Give students the responsibility of solving the problem.** Hands-on inquiry implies that students should be responsible for solving a given problem. To some degree, you must withdraw once the lesson is under way and accept a higher level of student self-direction, confusion, and noise. The role of "facilitator" may be unfamiliar, but it is essential in order to tap the true value of the inquiry approach. You must also ensure that all materials and resources that might be required by students in the course of the inquiry experience are available or attainable. In this manner, students are further enabled to approach problems independently.

- **Offer feedback and guidance.** Students, especially younger children or those new to inquiry, require both individual and group feedback and guidance on a regular basis. Your feedback can make students aware of the strategies and ideas they are developing and applying. You must also strike the delicate

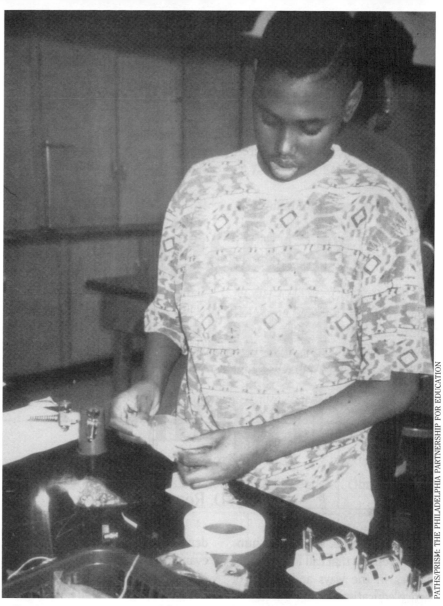

PATHS/PRISM: THE PHILADELPHIA PARTNERSHIP FOR EDUCATION

Effective management can shape chaotic hands-on inquiry into real learning.

balance between the chances for student success on one hand and the level of student dependence on the other hand. Finding this balance hinges on students' abilities, their familiarity with the method, and the nature of the problem under study.

- **Debrief.** Reserve time after the inquiry activity to evaluate the experience thoroughly. Through discussion, you can tie the results of the lesson to the ongoing classroom curriculum and explore the variety of student approaches and findings. This debriefing also provides an ideal forum for students to learn from each other and for you to asses their progress and build on their understanding.

- **Anticipate, prevent, monitor, and adapt.** Anticipate the range of management problems that might arise and then take whatever steps are necessary to prevent them. Be actively involved and ever vigilant, monitoring classroom activity throughout the lesson. This will allow you to identify and respond to any difficulties before they escalate. Adapt to any problems that arise once the lesson is under way, but keep the focus on the activity. Responding flexibly with "on the spot" management decisions is a regular aspect of life in the hands-on, inquiry classroom.

Teaching Risk-taking

Encouraging teachers to move away

from traditional methods of teaching science to more student-centered, open-ended methods is not easy. The most persuasive reports, the most compelling data, and the most articulate advocates will do little to calm the very real and reasonable anxieties teachers may have. Instead, it is essential that inservice and preservice teachers witness firsthand the power of a well-managed, hands-on, inquiry classroom to inspire students and motivate them toward meaningful learning.

Naturalistic observations, modeling, demonstrations, and case-study videotapes can provide convincing evidence of the potential of these methods. Then, teachers need to try hands-on activities in a risk-free workshop or small, supportive teaching environment. With sensitive, insightful peer feedback and continued trials, the management principles for inquiry methods will become routine. Teachers can then confidently begin shifting their classroom orientation to include active, investigative, student-centered methods in their instructional repertoire.

J. Richard Suchman wrote, "Inquiry is more than a method of science. Inquiry is science. It is at the center of the scientific way of life" (1968). Hands-on inquiry should also be central to our science teaching. By demystifying the risk associated with the technique, we can encourage more teachers to try hands-on inquiry in their classrooms.

Resources

Suchman, J.R. (1968). *Developing inquiry in Earth Science.* Chicago, IL: Science Research Associates.

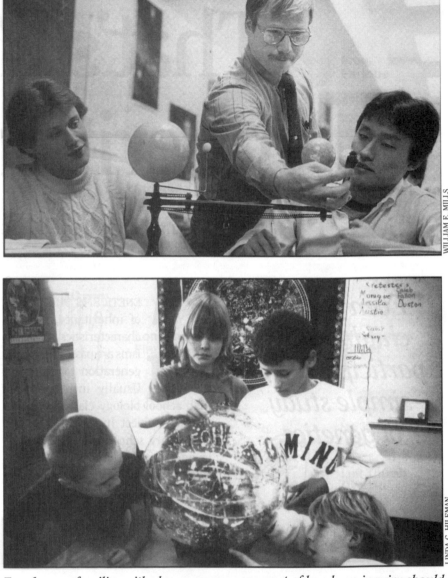

Teachers unfamiliar with classroom management of hands-on inquiry should first gain confidence doing activities in a risk-free, supportive setting. Then they can try the technique with their own students.

Additional Topic Resources

Lehman, J.R. (1992). Preservice problem solving. *Science and Children,* 29 (4), 30-31.

Orlich, D.C. (1989). Science inquiry and the commonplace. *Science and Children,* 26(6), 22-24

ALAN D. ROSSMAN, formerly associate director for teacher education at Northwestern University, now supervises science programs for children, adults, and teachers at the Chicago Botanic Garden.

Science Discovery Centers

By Mark D. Guy and Jackie Wilcox

"Cool!" "This is fun!" "I wonder what would happen if ...?" "Why does it do that?" "Can I try it again?" These are the words preservice teachers want to hear from their elementary students. The *National Science Education Standards* (National Research Council, 1996) emphasize experiences for teachers that integrate theory and practice with children in school settings.

In our elementary science methods course, preservice teachers create Science Discovery Centers—activity centers that teach a fundamental science concept through active interaction with materials—and present them at nearby schools. This assignment promotes authentic learning experiences consistent with the Standards and allows the preservice teachers to actively explore and reflect upon their science teaching and learning experiences.

Creating the Centers

Each preservice teacher creates a Science Discovery Center. The preservice teachers begin with an elementary science topic that interests them and select engaging hands-on activities they can use to teach the topic.

Preservice teachers design hands-on activity stations and present them for a field experience at a local elementary school

A preservice teacher guides two students at a center on static electricity.

The completed discovery center includes hands-on activities and a display with pictures, diagrams, and thought-provoking questions. (See Figure 1 for Science Discovery Center instructions.)

The preservice teachers present their centers at a Science Discovery Center Day at a local elementary school. They will also use the centers later in the year in their individual field experience classrooms.

While the classroom teachers at the elementary school we will be visiting have not been involved in planning the discovery centers, we make sure that a wide variety of topics are covered. Because so many different grade levels visit the centers, there have been many curricular connections for each class. This year, we are beginning to involve the classroom teachers more by asking for a list of desired topics ahead of time and matching centers with particular classes.

On a predetermined date, the preservice teachers set up their centers in a gymnasium or empty classroom at the elementary school. There are generally about 25 centers. Following a prearranged schedule (see Figure 2), classes of students visit the centers in small groups of two or three. Students spend 10–15 minutes at a center before moving on to another one. Primary-grade students visit centers designed for their age group, while intermediate-grade students visit centers designed for them. Students are able to visit four to five centers before the next classes arrive.

The preservice teachers conduct their center activities numerous times with students of varying abilities, interests, and ages. Therefore, the preservice teachers have the opportunity to guide and observe a variety of young learners actively "doing science" and adapt the activity either during or after each presentation. Each preservice teacher later completes a reflection paper describing how the students interacted with the discovery center and any revisions that are needed. Group interviews are also conducted shortly after the experience.

Center Examples

The Science Discovery Centers cover a wide variety of elementary science topics. For example, a center on flowers included an activity in which chil-

dren examined flowers discarded by a floral shop using hand lenses and a microscope. They collected pollen grains on a microscope slide for close examination. Students made drawings of their observations and learned the names of various parts of the flower. Discussion also included the interrelationship between flowering plants and pollination vectors such as bees and butterflies.

At a center on static electricity, students charged balloons, combs, or other plastic objects and observed the consequences. Children investigated the concept of similar charges repelling and dissimilar charges attracting. Discussion of their findings led to connections of static electricity to

> ### *Figure 1. Science Discovery Center Assignment.*
>
> **1.** Select an elementary science topic that interests you.
>
> **2.** Locate several activities that teach the concept. Use library and Internet resources for ideas. Look in particular for activities that use everyday materials.
>
> **3.** Select an engaging activity or activities that would last about 10 minutes, including setup and cleanup.
>
> **4.** Gather materials (be sure to have plenty on hand).
>
> **5.** Prepare a captivating display that shows a title and questions or directions.
>
> **6.** Be prepared to work with students of different ages and ability levels.
>
> **7.** Think about your role in letting the students explore.
>
> **8.** Be ready for action!

everyday life: static cling, "shocking" someone after rubbing feet on carpet, and lightning.

Another center on sedimentary and metamorphic rocks allowed students to create a model sedimentary rock and then change it into a metamorphic rock. Students layered bread, peanut butter, and jelly into a sandwich and compacted it slightly. The sandwich was sliced in half to show the layers of a sedimentary rock. Half the sandwich was then placed in a plastic bag, and by applying intense pressure (squeezing and squishing the bag), the children simulated a metamorphic rock. Students also observed samples of sedimentary and metamorphic rocks.

Other discovery center topics have included the five senses, seeds, simple machines, sinking and floating, fossils, and earthquakes.

A Learning Experience

The elementary students are so excited to explore the activities at each center. They are also attentive and focused on the concepts. The centers arouse the students' curiosity to actively investigate the science phenomena involved. The children's reactions are extremely positive both in terms of laughter and excitement as well as intellectual stimulation. Classroom teachers have reported that the children want to talk about their discovery center experience for several hours after their session is over.

The classroom teachers were impressed with the quality and variety of topics. They saw this as a valuable exchange between the preservice teachers and their own students. They especially liked the simple yet exciting hands-on activities and were pleased that centers reinforced concepts they taught in the classroom (as we mentioned earlier, we are now making more curricular connections by asking the classroom teachers for suggested topics). Some felt it gave their students a chance to apply their knowledge of the science concepts and to see firsthand how projects can demonstrate student knowledge. Some of the teachers even asked to borrow center ideas for their own classroom. After the visit, diagrams and descriptions of all center activities were sent to the teachers.

So far, principals at six different schools have been extremely supportive. They see the immediate advantages to their students and teachers, and they also think highly of the outreach effort and collaboration between their school and our college in the preparation of prospective elementary teachers. As one principal noted, "I wish you could come here every month." Others have asked, "How do I get on the list to have this activity at my school?" Some see how this type of event could be incorporated into a parent's night at the school.

Benefits to Participants

From the reflection papers and group interviews, it is clear that preservice teachers view the assignment as a valuable learning opportunity.

Realistic Experience. For many preservice teachers, the discovery center sessions were the first opportunities they had with "real" children in science. They were able to see their activity come to life in the hands and minds of the young learners. A common theme, "I liked the interaction with the students!" was woven throughout the reflection papers and the conversations with the participants. The preservice teachers saw the experience as more realistic than teaching their peers. For some students, the experience helped them become more confident to teach science.

Exciting Learning. The preservice teachers liked the excitement, interest, and curiosity they observed among the students who visited their centers. After presenting their activities to 10 to 12 different student groups, they were able to view how a variety of students react to science. The preservice teachers were able to obtain firsthand knowledge about the understandings different age students bring to a concept. They were able to directly observe different patterns of

Figure 2. Science Discovery Center Day Schedule.

8:15–9:00 A.M.	Preservice teachers arrive and set up (25 centers)
9:00–9:45 A.M.	Session One—four classes (grades K–1, rotate every 10 minutes)
9:45–10:00 A.M.	Break
10:00–10:45 A.M.	Session Two—four classes (grades 2–3, rotate every 10 minutes)
10:45–11:00 A.M.	Break
11:00–11:45 A.M.	Session Three—five classes (grades 4–5, rotate every 10 minutes)
11:45 A.M.– 12:00 NOON	Clean up and return to campus

behavior related to age level and student interest.

Adapting Activities. The preservice teachers learned to adapt activities to meet the needs of the different ages and abilities of the children they were teaching. Some of them even developed different activities based upon what children in previous groups had discovered. One preservice teacher decided that if she were more enthusiastic, the children would become more involved. It worked! Another changed her approach once she found that the children were reluctant to get involved without direction. She began to use different ways to motivate the various groups. Yet another discovered that her introductory activity distracted students away from the concept she was trying to present, so she used it later or not at all. She also had two groups complete all the activities at her center in a short time and had to formulate a question that fostered further investigation.

Shifting Role. Many preservice teachers noted that, in the course of the day, they shifted their teaching role to more of a facilitator than they had originally planned. Early on, many of them wanted to "show and tell" the students about the science concept at their center before they let them "do" it. They also reported a desire to direct the students step by step through the activity. As different groups visited their centers, however, many of the preservice teachers became more and more willing to let the students explore and investigate on their own. In turn, the young students responded more eagerly to the activity. One preservice teacher commented, "The first couple of times I did it, I told the children what to do. Later, I tended to let groups figure it out on their own, what was going to happen and make guesses as to why it happened. They enjoyed it a lot more, and I think they learned more than when I told them how it was supposed to work."

This year, the preservice teachers will take a break from teaching their own centers during one of the sessions and follow a group of children from center to center. This will allow the teachers to observe the activities at other centers and, more important, closely observe how the children engage in various activities and demonstrate conceptual understandings.

The discovery center experience reinforced many ideas presented in class regarding the importance of exploration, the teacher as facilitator, and how simple materials can promote exciting thought among young learners. For several preservice teachers, the experience affirmed their desire to become a teacher and engage in exciting science encounters with their future students. It also allowed prospective teachers to be both actively engaged as learners and to reflect on their own growth in becoming effective science teachers (Raizen and Michelsohn, 1994). On a practical note, one preservice teacher offered this insight: "I think this gave us an accurate picture of what teaching is like and how much work goes into teaching a successful lesson."

From this high-energy experience, preservice teachers see how hands-on science can be fun and exciting for young learners. This aspect of elementary science is valuable but represents only a first step in becoming an effective science teacher. More important, the preservice teachers have the opportunity to experience directly two subtle yet powerful instructional strategies related to teaching inquiry-based science: adapting the lesson to address student needs and consciously shifting their teaching role to more of a facilitator.

Resources

National Research Council. (1996). *National Science Education Standards.* Washington, DC: National Academy Press.

Raizen, S.A., and Michelsohn, A.M. (1994). *The Future of Science in Elementary Schools: Educating Prospective Teachers.* San Francisco: Jossey-Bass Publishers.

Also in S&C

Cullinan, K. (1995). Recharge yourself at a science center. (Teaching Teachers) *Science and Children, 33*(3), 41–42.

Tennies, R.H., and Thielk, C.K. (1997). The science advocate. *Science and Children, 34*(5), 30–31, 40.

MARK D. GUY is an assistant professor and JACKIE WILCOX is a doctoral candidate, both in the Department of Teaching and Learning at the University of North Dakota in Grand Forks.

Talk Less, Say More

Silence can be a powerful tool for student understanding

By Mary Dickinson Bird

"TALK LESS, SAY MORE." It's a piece of New England folk wisdom that takes on special meaning for my class of preservice elementary teachers.

I teach in an environment of collaborative exploration, where students share struggles and triumphs and see themselves as part of a community of science learning. Through active laboratory and field experiences we investigate unfamiliar science concepts and build new skills, reflecting on each experience while expanding curiosity, confidence, imagination, and joy in our approach to science. It's an exciting—and noisy—process!

Incorporating a period of carefully planned silence in the midst of this lively adventure can be a tremendously powerful tool for understanding. It gives students the opportunity to test ideas and relate to one another in an entirely different way and often leads them to new insights.

That's why early in each semester, I challenge my students to tackle a team project in which they may use any form of communication *except speech*. Students must analyze a problem and collaboratively develop and test possible solutions *without talk-*

ing. The process they use during this project often changes their preconceived ideas about themselves and each other and about scientific knowledge and problem solving.

Through this experience students compare ideas, strategize, compete, and confer within and among groups in new ways. For the students the

Students must analyze a problem and collaboratively develop and test possible solutions *without talking*.

experience can be transforming. For me the activity provides a valuable perspective on the relationships among students, teacher, and subject matter.

Free Exploration

When the students enter the classroom on the day of the project, each table is set with a 6–10 L plastic dish tub and an assortment of corks, metal washers, wooden craft sticks, string, film canisters, marbles, clay, plastic straws, rubber bands, a small square of aluminum foil, and other objects.

The assortment varies somewhat from table to table, but all have at least one thing in common: an iron ball measuring 4 cm in diameter. (I found a whole bin of these balls in my classroom when I came here; large fishing weights would work equally well.)

I divide students into groups of four or five students each and have them fill the tubs two-thirds full of water. Most students quickly decide to test their materials for sinkers and floaters, even though our class hasn't yet considered these materials or concepts formally. Soon other groups join in. The students chatter and converse. Students observe that washers sink quickly to the bottom or the tub, poker chips drift down slowly, and plastic berry baskets—full of holes—float. Large paper clips sink, small ones float.

Inevitably, some students start trying to "turn" sinkers into floaters and floaters into sinkers—a metal washer dropped in water by itself sinks, but floats when it is placed gently on the floating foil square. Similarly, a craft stick girdled by a chunk of clay sinks, yet a piece of clay molded into a cuplike shape stays afloat.

Again, there is lively banter as students swap ideas, and I record their ideas on the chalkboard. The students

LINDA OLLIVER

are fairly certain that size, shape, and weight of objects have something to do with whether they sink or float. Because they haven't figured out the relationships among these features, they are puzzled by the failure of some of their assumptions, especially the floating paper clips, clay, and berry basket, and the sinking rubber bands.

Vocabulary learned years ago begins to emerge: *density, buoyancy, surface tension.* Though we later explore the meaning of the terms, we don't discuss them at this point. In my experience, mastery of scientific-sounding words can sometimes fool the listener (and speaker) into mistaking facility with language for conceptual understanding.

Some students think if they understand the term, they are finished with the difficult, thinking part of an investigation. Other students, less con-fident with the vocabulary, give up before they have mastered the important concepts. Many students have been schooled to equate the use of a scientific term with conceptual understanding and closure of an investigation—my failure to grant any special status to these words signals students that we are far from finished and there is much to understand.

Welcome to Silencia

Some teachers and administrators argue that "free" exploration and conversation take valuable time from formal instruction, but I disagree. I believe David Hawkins (1974) was right when he wrote that learners need the luxury of investigating on their own and "to cross the line between ignorance and insight many times" to develop genuine understanding.

After "playing" with the materi-

als, students are relaxed and inquisitive, ready to take on an unusual challenge. At this point I place a laminated instruction sheet on each table. As the students follow along, I read it aloud:

Welcome to the island nation of Silencia.

You and your fellow villagers enjoy a tropical paradise with all the resources you need to support your existence. Your neighbors to the west, however, are not so lucky. The island of Flotensia is in trouble. Their crops have failed, and the island residents are in danger of starving.

You can help save them. The fruit of the ironball tree is nutritious and plentiful on Silencia. But you and your fellow villagers will have to figure out a way to transport the fruit across to Flotensia—not an easy task, since the fruit is as dense and heavy as its name suggests and also rots immediately upon contact with water. (There is an example of ironball fruit in your tub.)

Using materials available on your island (the items in the tub), devise a vessel that can transport the ironball fruit safely across the channel (the tub) to Flotensia.

Feel free to trade materials and ideas with other Silencia villages.

Oh, by the way: The reason your island is named "Silencia" is that none of the villagers can speak.

From this moment on, no one is allowed to talk. Students in each group look at each other with a mixture of amusement, confusion, delight, and frustration. For some it seems like a joke at first, for others an intriguing challenge, and for still others another bit of evidence that their teacher is an alien. I see students surveying the materials on their tables, questioning each other with their eyes. Then someone reaches for the iron ball and a piece of foil, and the quest has begun.

Communication in Many Ways

It is interesting to work my way around the room and observe what's happening. In one group a girl struggles to tie two film canisters together. A teammate catches on to the raft idea and quickly lends a hand to its construction. Others in the group offer materials in anticipation of their need.

In the next group two students are sitting in frustration as another fends off their attempts to help with his foil boat design. One teammate drums the table with anxious fingers, eyeing the pile of materials. An idea is clearly simmering here, but it has not yet boiled over.

A third group has abandoned the idea of a boat altogether. Two students are busy rigging a sling for the iron ball as the other two construct a pulley system with string and film canisters. They plan to haul the cargo across the channel, above the water's surface! (Remember, the challenge said nothing about *floating* the fruit from Silencia to Flotensia!)

Groups vary in the ways they develop and test their ideas. Some students experiment with component parts on the way to a complete design, choosing and discarding elements, making refinements at every step. Others don't go near the water

until their entire vessel is built. Some groups have multiple designs under construction, simultaneously or in rapid succession. These groups flit from idea to idea in what could be careless haste, a superficial knowledge of critical concepts, or sometimes a quick grasp of the problem.

Throughout the process students find myriad ways to communicate. A few begin by writing everything down, but soon discover how laborious this strategy is. Before long they are gesticulating, wiggling eyebrows, grunting, and nodding with their teammates. Eye contact takes on great importance and facial expressions are dramatic.

It is interesting to see how "cultural transmission" occurs (or doesn't occur) among the groups. Usually students begin the activity as though it is a competition, despite instructions that clearly encourage sharing. They position their bodies to shield their work from others' view, glare at "spies" from other groups, and so on. However, once one group arrives at a successful design, at least a couple more opt to imitate or improve upon it. Other groups continue doggedly on the quest for a unique solution.

Often it is only after one group achieves success that students begin to eye their colleagues with trading in mind. One team barters away all its film canisters for a handful of plastic foam packing peanuts. Another group swaps string and rubber bands for all the foil and plasticine it can find. Yet another team looks beyond the tub contents and begins scavenging around the classroom. This group has deduced that, because I am obeying

the law of silence, then I must be a village trading partner, too, and my supplies are available for their use.

The subsequent designs are created with imagination and determination, and they indicate a growing awareness that more is needed to succeed than just knowledge of what sinks and floats. Students experiment with various ways to keep their rolling cargo stable and begin to consider distribution of weight and center of mass as they discover the peril of carrying heavy cargo "on deck." One group discovers neutral buoyancy and realizes it is possible to create a submarine to carry the iron ball. The team with the pulley and sling system has opened a world of mechanical possibilities.

Thanks to a scheduled three-hour block of laboratory and seminar time, I have the luxury of allowing the investigation to continue until all groups have designed a solution to the problem, as quick as 15–20 minutes for some groups to about an hour for every group to find a solution. Those who experience quick initial success are challenged to create a second or third solution. This often turns out to be a profitable exercise for it enables students to explore their understanding of critical concepts.

Let the Voices Begin

When every team has found at least one solution, we celebrate with a round of applause. Then I invite students to comment on the investigation. Students are eager to talk about the designs, the design process, and the nature of the interactions that occurred. We discuss the features of the various vessels and consider what made them successful or disastrous. At this point students consider the list of vocabulary words generated earlier and begin to use the words with real meaning.

I ask the students to reflect on how they worked as teams to meet this challenge. Typically, students share such comments as, "It was harder than we expected" and "Everyone contributed, and we all took turns!" and "We thought we knew what would sink and float, but making this boat made us throw out everything that we knew."

It doesn't take much probing for students to realize that the dynamics in this activity are unusual. A group leader might have been in charge at the start, but often it's a quieter student whose ideas are more compelling. When every student is silent, no one's voice dominates. This seems to extend to nonverbal behavior as well, for even in groups where someone starts out as a "materials hog," the rest of the group eventually asserts itself and insists on full, equal participation.

Often students report that the leadership role rotates throughout the entire group as design ideas evolve. The effects of this power shift endure throughout the semester.

In addition to considering conceptual understanding and group dynamics, students also reflect on their gen-

eral approach to learning and problem solving in the follow-up discussion. Many students realize their attitudes toward risk and failure have undergone a change. Students' feelings of frustration when their ships sank are tempered by a genuine sense of pride and accomplishment in finding workable designs. They are not embarrassed about their failures or those of their colleagues and are quick to point out that, almost inevitably, it was someone's mistake that led each group to a better idea.

It also does not escape the students' notice that *time* has been essential to the development of ideas and relationships in this investigation: time to figure out how to communicate, time to test designs and learn from mistakes, time to make sense of their understanding, time to learn how to lead and follow and share. Time is not a luxury, but a necessity.

Working in silence during this time gives students a rare opportunity to explore concepts and build understanding unfettered by established patterns of communication and leadership. The silence helps students tap new problem-solving resources in themselves and their peers. Quiet students safely emerge from the shadow of shyness, while students who tend to dominate discussion learn to attend more closely to their classmates. Mistakes become much more productive, because in the silence they are

just little steps on the way to learning, not echoing embarrassments.

These experiences and reflections provide my students and me with much to consider as we explore opportunities for science success throughout the remainder of the term. I am confident that my students have enriched their understanding of important concepts, become stronger colleagues and problem solvers, and are more tolerant of failure as a necessary, time-consuming step toward success.

For most students, especially the science-shy, this opportunity to lead and succeed is invaluable. It provides the empowerment they need to believe they can do—and teach—elementary science. In this instance, by talking less, we have said a great deal indeed!

Mary Dickinson Bird is an instructor of science and environmental education in the College of Education and Human Development at the University of Maine in Orono.

Resources

Hawkins, D. (1974). Messing about in science. In *The Informed Vision: Essays on Learning and Human Nature* (pp. 65–75). New York: Agathon.

Never Give 'Em a Straight Answer

By Charlotte Ward

There is nothing more provoking than asking a question and getting another question in reply, and that is why I recommend this method of the teaching/learning of science at every level, from kindergarten through college. Science begins and ends with questions. Well, almost—you have to notice things before you can ask about them.

Babies make their parents' hearts rejoice as they notice more and more things in their surroundings. They reach for a finger, smile back at a smiling face, bat at a mobile toy to set it in motion, and cry when they need attention. They are asking questions of their environment, finding out what people and objects will do in response.

Unfortunately, when children learn to talk and begin asking an endless stream of questions of parents and other adults, they are often rebuffed. Realistically, one cannot stop and answer every question instantly, but if children's questions about the world around them are seldom or never answered by the important adults in their lives, they come to the reasonable conclusion that questioning is

not important. By the middle school years, perhaps earlier, they have quit asking, and even quit observing the world around them.

For nearly 30 years, I taught an introductory physical science course intended to prepare elementary education students to teach science. One of my greatest frustrations was trying to find common observations my students had made that I could use to make connections with the scientific principles I needed to teach. Were these students not observant because they were not "scientifically inclined" or because their powers of observation and sense of wonder had never been encouraged? I find that, whatever the reason, many individuals go through life with blinders on. I'm not trying to make scientists out of them; I just think they are missing a great deal of life.

Encouraging Wonder

So how do we, as science teachers, encourage our students to notice their environment in the broadest sense? Here is where I believe the Socratic method, the provoking technique of

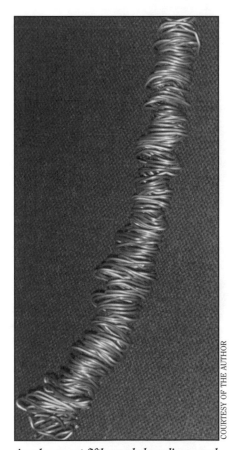

An observant fifth-grade boy discovered this twisted mass of wire at the bus stop. With questioning, he realized that it had been created by a tornado that passed through the night before.

STEVE BUHMAN

When a child asks a question such as "How high is the flagpole?" teachers should reply "I don't know. How can we find out?"

answering a question with a question, can help.

A story of a famous ichthyologist who taught at Harvard University in the mid-nineteenth century illustrates the method I am recommending. It seems that when a new graduate student applied to work with Louis Agassiz, the great naturalist would take the student into the laboratory, give him a preserved fish specimen, and tell him to study it until Agassiz returned.

The student would give the fish a casual once-over, expecting the professor to return in an hour or so, but in fact, the student would not see him again until the next day. Agassiz would then question the student briefly about the observations—just enough to convince the student that there was more to be learned from looking at the fish than previously imagined. This was likely to go on for several days, with the student having no assignment except to look at the fish. At the end of that time, what began as

sheer boredom would have resulted not only in an intimate and detailed knowledge of that fish, but also a lively curiosity about fish in general—or else a different choice of life's work.

Probably none of us can imagine taking Agassiz's approach today. We'd think we didn't have that kind of time. Moreover, each day we are assaulted with so many stimuli we have to turn most of them off in self-defense. How, then, can we encourage our students to observe their world so they are able to question and understand it, not only in preparation for careers in science, but also simply to enhance their enjoyment and well-being in a world where they can feel at home?

Questioning Pendulums

Let us look at a couple of examples I use with my preservice teaching students in which a series of questions can help them not only to observe, but also to organize their observations in ways that lead to a conclusion that

can be tested, either by experimentation or with information that is already available.

The first, which can be used with children as young as fourth grade, is a sort of microcosmic view of the scientific method. I call it "playing Galileo." I begin by telling students the (probably true) story of Galileo and the swinging candelabra in the church at Pisa. The candelabra, perhaps set in motion by a breeze, was swaying back and forth. Galileo became entranced with watching its slowly dying motion. He began to measure, with his pulse, the time it took for the candelabra to complete one swing. Like any careful experimenter, he made the measurement several times. Although the width (amplitude) of the swings differed considerably, he was always (within the limits of accuracy of his method) getting the same time for every complete swing.

You would think that the distance the candelabra traveled would determine the time required for the swing. Galileo did. But that wasn't the case. He had noticed an unexpected behavior of the swinging candelabra. Then he asked the crucial question: If the distance traveled doesn't determine the period (time for one round trip) of the candelabra, what does?

Now we get to the crux of the experimental method: making the system (the thing we study) as simple as possible and ferreting out the individual factors that might affect its behavior. My students and I decide, as Galileo did, that the large, ornate candelabra is basically just a mass on a string—a pendulum. So we make a pendulum by tying a small, dense "bob" on a thin string, hanging it on a hook so that it can swing freely, and observing its properties. I ask, "What are they?" The teachers will soon see that there are only two: the mass of the bob and the length of the string.

The bob contributes almost nothing to the length, and the string contributes almost nothing to the mass. For simplicity's sake, we ignore those negligible contributions. Learning to decide what can safely be ignored is a crucial part of a scientist's training.

If that's all there is to a pendulum, then its period must depend on the mass, the length, or both. That's our hypothesis: The period of a pendulum depends on its mass, its length, or both. I ask students, "How can we find out which it is?" Someone will surely suggest that we observe bobs of different masses and strings of different lengths. Someone also ought to suggest that we'd better change only one thing at a time—the fancy name for that is "isolating the variables."

The hard part, planning the experiment to test the hypothesis, has now been done. Now students just get a couple of pieces of string that differ quite a bit in length, two or three small bobs of different masses, and a timer that is more reliable than Galileo's "pulse" method, such as a watch with a second hand. If you don't already know how the experiment comes out, you now have enough information to find out for yourself.

A "Burning" Question

My second example for the students deals with a chemical question. Humans began to use fire nearly half a million years ago, but the solution to the mystery of the process we call "burning" is barely two centuries old. When something burns, such as a log of wood on a campfire, the ash that remains is smaller in volume and lighter in mass than the original log. When something burns, part or all of it disappears. I ask my students, "Is this always the case?"

I ask, "What if we burn a piece of steel wool?" To be sure if some of it disappears, we weigh it first. After all the sparkling is over, we have a pile of gray powder left. We weigh it. Uh-oh! The powder is heavier than the steel wool we started with. I ask, "What could cause that?"

Children are usually taught at an early age that if their clothes catch fire, they should grab a blanket and wrap it around them to smother the flames (to keep out the oxygen). They may have learned how to gently nurse a campfire into life by fanning (providing extra oxygen). These observations suggest that burning might involve something in the air—something invisible, but nonetheless real. I ask "How can we find out?"

They might reply that we could try burning something, such as a candle, in a closed jar. If the candle goes out, something in the air must have been used up. I ask, "Where did it go?"

If air is a real—although invisible—thing, maybe wood and candles turn into invisible products when they burn instead of simply disappearing. Some gases, water vapor for instance, turn to liquid when cooled. We hold a saucer full of ice cubes over our burning candle, making sure the bottom of the saucer is dry. We watch for a minute or two. I ask, "Where did the water on the bottom of the saucer come from?" and "What do these observations suggest about what happens when materials burn?"

These two examples of using questions to prompt observation and direct experimentation are adaptable to classrooms at many levels, and they can be used under controlled conditions to teach the methods and practice of science. But think of the countless questions sparked by everyday situations that can start the same kind of process of learning.

Beyond the Classroom

Teachers are often nervous that they may not know the answer to a child's question. In that case, the proper reply should be, "I don't know. How do you think we can find out?" The answer to that question might be as straightforward as, "We could look it up in the library or check the Internet."

One recent summer evening, just at dusk, my husband called me over to the kitchen door to see something interesting. We watched a spider build an intricate orb web across the corner of the roof over the back stoop. It took about an hour to build the web. We checked several times before we went to bed to see if the spider was catching anything. It was—several insects were ensnared in the web. Next morning, however, the web was gone. We supposed a bird had eaten the spider.

To our amazement, the spider was back the next night—at least it looked like the same spider—building another web in the same place. Next morning, it was gone again. This happened several more nights. What was going on here? Finally, I got up early enough, just at first light, to solve the mystery. As dawn broke, the spider ate the web filament completely and apparently went into a crevice of the roof to spend the day. That sent me to the library to read more about spiders, and to learn that what I had observed for the first time in my rather long life was normal behavior for several species of spiders.

Paying attention to a small thing, a spider spinning a web, led to an adventure in learning. My discovery was of no great consequence. I won't win a Nobel prize for something arachnid experts have known for years. But it added to my appreciation and enjoyment of the world I live in. By encouraging students to wonder, observe, and question, we can introduce all our students to new possibilities for enjoying their world.

Also in S&C

Lehman, J.R. (1992). Preservice problem solving. *Science and Children, 28*(7), 44–47.

Otto, P.B. (1991). Finding an answer in questioning strategies. *Science and Children, 29*(4), 30–31.

Spargo, P.E., and Enderstein, L.G. (1997). What questions do they ask? Ausubel rephrased. *Science and Children, 34*(6), 43–45.

CHARLOTTE WARD is an associate professor of physics emerita at Auburn University in Alabama. She taught physical science for elementary education majors for 25 years and still conducts science day camps for fourth-through sixth-grade students.

Resources

- "NSTA recommends" at *www.nsta.org/recommends,* a searchable website of popular reviews of science-teaching materials

- **SC*L*INKS.**
  THE WORLD'S A CLICK AWAY

  Topic: Science Method
  Go to: *www.scilinks.org*
  Code: PAE01